NAPOLEON

Born: August 15, 1769
Died: May 5, 1821

The fascinating story of Napoleon Bonaparte, military genius and master of tactical warfare, his meteoric rise from an obscure officer to Commander of the Grand Army of France, Emperor and absolute monarch of half of Europe. The Little Corporal, born on the island of Corsica of poor peasant stock, became a hero when he routed the British fleet at Toulon and later quelled the rioting mobs of Paris. He reorganized the economic structure of the nation, established the Bank of France, codified its laws in what later became known as the Napoleonic code, reopened churches and schools and extended the borders of France across the whole of Europe.

Books by Manuel Komroff

MARCO POLO
NAPOLEON
JULIUS CAESAR
THOMAS JEFFERSON

MANUEL KOMROFF

NAPOLEON

JULIAN MESSNER, INC.   NEW YORK

Published by Julian Messner, Inc.
8 West 40th Street, New York 18

Published Simultaneously in Canada
By The Copp Clark Company, Ltd.

Library of Congress Catalog Card No. 54-10590

Eighth Printing, 1963

CONTENTS

CONTENTS

For My Nephew
BOYD

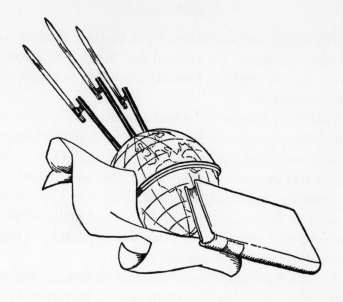

I

A WHIFF OF GRAPESHOT

Two years after Louis XVI, the King of France, had mounted the scaffold of the guillotine, the Revolutionary Government found itself in grave danger. The same impassioned mobs that had swept the Revolution into power now threatened to destroy its governing body.

The streets of Paris resounded with angry cries, "Down with the Convention!" "Down with the Constitution!" "Long live the King!"

The frightened shopkeepers put up their shutters and barred their doors. They feared that the Reign of Terror, which had steeped the French Revolution in blood, was about to return.

This time, however, the mobs in the streets were not marching against the King and a corrupt aristocracy; they were marching against the National Convention, which was their own revolutionary government made up of specially appointed delegates. They had become impatient of the many unavoidable delays and critical of the proposed constitution. They were agitating to overthrow their new government.

But the National Convention, true to the spirit of the Revolution, was determined to use all its power in an effort to establish a peaceful democratic regime and bring to the people of France a constitution establishing their civil rights. Therefore, at four-thirty in the morning of October 3, 1795, after a stormy meeting, it appointed Barras, a deputy leader devoted to democracy, to take all necessary measures to defend Paris and the Revolutionary Government.

At this early hour, before dawn, Barras, now Director of Defense, desperately casting about for some military man capable of meeting this critical situation, suddenly thought of the siege of Toulon. He remembered how the victory of this battle was due entirely to the skill and brilliance of a young unknown artillery officer named Napoleon Bonaparte. He remembered how this young

10

captain of artillery, only twenty-six years old, had arrived in Toulon and in a few months' time had risen to the rank of general.

Suddenly Barras turned to those about him and said, "I have just the man we need. He is a little Corsican officer who will not stand upon ceremony."

Then, going to his desk, Barras wrote quickly. "Citizen Bonaparte is requested to be at Chaillot at 10:00 A.M. tomorrow, to meet Citizen Director Barras on urgent business. Greeting and Brotherhood."

*   *   *

Napoleon's interview with Barras was very brief.

"Paris is ablaze. Can the city be defended?"

"Yes," replied the young officer.

"As Director of Defense I appoint you to take command."

Without a word Napoleon saluted his superior and left the room.

He hurried through the streets of Paris back to his barracks. There was no time to be lost. He knew that the mobs were already armed and organized. He knew that they numbered twenty-five thousand men. And he also knew that at that moment all the troops in the Paris garrisons amounted to only five thousand men. He was now in command of these five thousand. How could five thousand hold out against twenty-five thousand? There was only one way. Cannon!

Arriving at the barracks, Napoleon ordered Major Murat and his horsemen to race to a place five miles off, where fifty cannons were posted. It was urgent that they get there as fast as possible, before the mob could take possession of this artillery. And, as it happened, Murat and his fast horsemen arrived just in time. A mob armed with muskets, knives and clubs was already on its way to capture these fifty cannons.

A few minutes' delay and all would have been lost. A few minutes' delay and history would have been different. Only a slight delay and Napoleon might never have been crowned Emperor of France.

But Murat and his men did arrive in time. And Napoleon used the fifty cannons to the greatest advantage. He ordered several mounted on the bridges of the Seine. In this way he secured command of both banks of the river and of the Palace of the Tuileries, which housed the government. He also mounted cannons in the avenues which led to the Tuileries and in the open square before the building. And, to add to these defenses, he posted several battalions in the palace gardens.

In very short time his defenses were ready. Now he awaited the attack.

At two o'clock in the afternoon the mobs began milling through the streets. They gathered from all directions and soon, twenty-five thousand strong, were marching toward the Tuileries. They were determined to capture the government.

Shouting and singing, they came closer and closer until they reached the streets leading directly to the palace. They crowded on toward their goal and it was then that Napoleon gave the order to fire. The cannons roared and the streets were raked with grapeshot. The mobs scattered in confusion. They fled, leaving the streets covered with dead and wounded. In a few minutes the action was over.

Now the government troops marched through Paris disarming the terrified inhabitants. Before nightfall the city was quiet and the National Convention secure from mob rule.

Full credit for this victory came to Barras, the Director of Defense, and to his "little Corsican officer." Barras was rewarded. He became Director in Chief of the government. But he did not forget that he owed everything to the young General Bonaparte.

Five days later Napoleon was named second-in-command of the Army of the Interior. And very soon after this, Barras, having had little military experience and finding his new duties most difficult, turned over the affairs of the army to the little general.

It was in this way that Napoleon, the twenty-six-year-old general, became Commander in Chief of the Army of the Interior. Never before had France had so young a general in full command.

A year before, hardly anyone in the whole land had heard of this young Corsican. Now, through a "whiff of grapeshot," the name Napoleon Bonaparte was known all over France. But while everyone spoke his name they all asked the same questions: "Who is he?" "Where has he come from?"

* * *

Napoleon was born on the island of Corsica on August 15, 1769. For centuries this mountainous island, situated in the Mediterranean about sixty miles off the coast of Italy, was the object of conquest. It had, at different periods, been conquered and ruled by the Phoenicians, Romans, Byzantines, Lombards, Franks and Genoese. Corsica was an island that possessed a long history of invasions.

And only three months before Napoleon's birth it was subjected to still another invasion. Prior to this it belonged to Genoa, but now it became a French possession. Thus Napoleon, while born in Corsica, was born on French soil.

Napoleon was the second son of eight children born to the Bonapartes. It was a family tradition that second sons should be named Napoleon.

He was a gentle, loving baby, but after the age of two he developed streaks of obstinacy. Even as a very small child he was masterful, determined and daring.

He himself confessed many years later that, as a boy, "Nothing impressed me. Nothing disturbed me. I was quarrelsome and combative and afraid of no one. I hit and scratched my companions, and they were all frightened of me. My brother Joseph had the worst time of all. I used to thump him and bite him. He was the one to be scolded, because by the time he recovered from his fright I was accusing him to my mother. It was a useful trick, for otherwise Mama Letizia would have punished me for fighting. She would never have allowed these attacks of mine."

So rough were his manners that when Napoleon was only five years old his mother sent him to a girls' school, thinking that gentle young girls would have a soothing influence on him. But the shy girls did not quiet his quarrelsome nature. And so he was sent to join his elder brother, Joseph, at a Jesuit school. Here he encountered strict routine and in time he learned to respect discipline. He began to discover the value of cooperation and self-control, although he was still subject to violent bursts of temper. And he was ever grateful to his old teacher in this school who had been so patient with him. Many years later, when he was Emperor, he rewarded this good Abbé Recco with the sum of twenty thousand francs for his understanding and "for teaching me to read."

Reading became the key to his future life. It was through books that Napoleon at a very early age saw a broad, wide world open before him. Through books the primitive little island of Corsica became, for the boy Napoleon, a mere dot on a vast unrolling chart. In books he found stories of ancient lands and nations that once ruled the world. He learned about other people, their habits, their history, their arts. From books he learned how oppressed people had risen against their conquerors. The history of his native Corsica alone was filled with examples of invasions, conquests and heroic liberations. Reading fired his imagination. What Caesar, Alexander and Charlemagne had accomplished, he too might someday achieve.

Napoleon's father was anxious that his sons should be educated, but since he was poor and could not afford the cost of good schools he made application for government scholarships. At that time it was the custom of the King of France, Louis XVI, to pay the expenses of a selected group of young boys to be educated in military academies. But all applicants were required to speak French and at this time Napoleon and his brother Joseph knew no language except their native Corsican. Their father, therefore, scraped together what money he could and sent Joseph and Napoleon, who was nine years old, to a school in Autun in southern France. Here they were to learn French as quickly as possible.

The few months that Napoleon spent in Autun were unhappy ones. In France everything was different from what he had known at home. Life in Corsica was quite primitive, but in France there was a refinement that stemmed from an old culture.

It was not easy for the boy Napoleon to act like a French gentleman. His peasant manners were not tolerated and he was obliged to conform, and to restrain his violent bursts of temper. He was also reminded by his schoolfellows that he belonged to a conquered people and often he was insulted and called a "slave." His tormentors jeered at his peculiar Corsican name, his foreign accent, his independent manner. The relations between himself and those about him were strained, and remained so during his entire stay in the school. He was alone. But he worked hard and was quick to learn.

Of these days in school there is the report of one of his teachers. "He was a sullen, melancholy boy during his early days at Autun. He refused to play with his schoolfellows, and usually walked to the school buildings quite alone. He had great ability, grasped things quickly and learned easily. When I gave him an hour's lesson, he used to stare at me, eyes and mouth wide open. But if ever I started to repeat what I had just said, he would answer coldly, almost bitterly, 'I know all that already.' "

Anything he heard once, he remembered. This marvelous memory contributed greatly to his later success. He remembered what he heard, what he read and what he saw. Later in life he remembered the names and faces of thousands of his soldiers and on the field of battle he knew exactly where each of his many cannons was placed.

After three and a half months at Autun, Napoleon could speak French quite fluently. He was now ready to enter the Military Academy of Brienne, where his father had succeeded in getting a scholarship for him.

In this school of one hundred and fifty boys, there were sixty who had scholarships from the King of France Here the boys learned Latin, French, German, history, literature, geography, mathematics, military science, catechism and drawing. Special hours were also set aside for fencing, singing, dancing and music. English was omitted because England was at that time an enemy of France. And although the boys spent long hours at work they also had plenty of exercise, fresh air and good food.

Napoleon showed marked ability in the subjects he liked. He was interested in history, both ancient and modern. He also liked geography, mathematics and military science. He filled his exercise books with many extracts that he copied out of the books he read. These passages inspired him and he copied them so that he could better remember them.

During his years at the academy Napoleon was not certain that he wanted to follow a military career. And at one time he even thought he would like to become a naval officer. But, when he learned that the French navy was most exclusive and that a boy with little money or influence would be hopelessly handicapped, he gave up this idea. And it was through the study of artillery, in which he took a passionate interest, that he was brought back to the idea of becoming a military officer.

Everything about the booming of big cannon fascinated him. He read all he could about artillery. And the more he read the more he wanted to learn. And it was because of this special interest that he decided to enter the Military College of France.

But this Military College, located in Paris, was a most expensive school. The boarding fees alone amounted to two thousand francs a year. However, there were a number of scholarships which poor boys might gain through competition. This was Napoleon's chance. He was determined that he would prove himself worthy. He worked hard and passed the examinations with high marks.

When young Napoleon arrived at the Military College in Paris he was fifteen years old. In his pocket he carried a letter of recommendation from his teachers. This letter described him as "an ambitious, commanding and strong-willed character." These were the very traits he had shown from infancy.

* * *

Napoleon arrived in Paris in the year 1784. In this year Louis XVI was on the throne of France and Marie Antoinette, an Austrian princess, was Queen. A few years before, France had come to the aid of the American Colonies and had sent Lafayette and four thousand soldiers to help General Washington.

Louis XVI did not help the American Revolution because of his love for liberty and democracy. He sent aid only because he wanted to see England, his enemy, defeated.

And England was defeated, but the spirit of liberty

and democracy, unchained by the success of the American Revolution, spread to France. And many reasoned that if the people of America could free themselves from tyranny then the people of France should do the same.

In the very year Napoleon entered the Military College in Paris, food riots broke out in a number of cities; and mobs gathered to protest against the high taxation which made life unbearable for the common people. These were times of trouble.

Early in that same year, Napoleon's father died, leaving his mother a widow with eight children. Napoleon considered his elder brother, Joseph, a weak person and so he appointed himself head of the familly. He immediately plunged into his work determined to learn everything he could of the science of war and to get his commission as quickly as possible so that no time would be lost in bringing assistance to his mother.

At sixteen, only one year after entering the Military College, he took his examinations and graduated with the rank of lieutenant.

During the next four years France was shaken by more hunger riots, more protests against crushing taxes, and even by open defiance against the King. And on July 14, 1789, the Bastille was stormed by a mob and the French Revolution was launched on its bloody and glorious course.

Napoleon, as a young officer of a battalion, was sent to various parts of France to help quell riots and disturbances. And the more he saw of active duty the more he was convinced that artillery held the key to victory in modern warfare. He, therefore, applied himself to his favorite subject, working out new problems and making himself a master of this branch of military science. He felt that artillery had been neglected and he was convinced that, since cannon could now be built larger and more powerful, it was of great importance.

He concentrated on this branch of the service and was soon elevated to captain of artillery. So great was his faith in cannon that once, when he was twenty-three and visiting in Paris, he valued cannon above the lives of the people or the justice of their cause. The Revolution was on in full force. A mob was storming the Tuileries and he followed it into the palace gardens to see what would happen. The uneasy King of France appeared on the palace balcony wearing the red cap of the Revolution. At this ridiculous sight Napoleon exclaimed to those about him, "Poor driveler! How can he suffer this rabble to enter? If he had swept away five or six hundred with his cannon, the rest would be running yet."

Regardless of the cost in human lives Napoleon never missed a chance to measure the effectiveness of artillery.

* * *

Three years after the fall of the Bastille the French army and navy abandoned the King and joined the Revolutionists. And the National Convention of the Revolution proclaimed France a Republic. But the French people did not gain their liberty without a great deal of bloodshed. Napoleon himself witnessed a second attack on the Tuileries in which five thousand people were killed by the soldiers of the King. And a month later in the streets of Paris he saw a massacre of twelve hundred people. Such slaughter occurred over and over again in all parts of France. But the people in revolt were not the only ones to shed their blood; many Royalists were guillotined. And others fled from France in terror. Even the King and his family attempted to escape, but they were arrested, returned to Paris and imprisoned.

However, the ideals of the Revolution did not take hold in all parts of France. A few regions, especially in the south, still supported the King and the aristocracy. In the Mediterranean port of Toulon the Royalists were strong enough to stage an insurrection and take control of the city.

At this point the English, who were in sympathy with the Royalists, sent their fleet into the harbor to help them capture the forts of the city that were in the hands of the Revolutionists.

It happened that at this time Napoleon, the young captain of artillery, was in Marseilles on a military mission and he was ordered to Toulon to take over the command of artillery in defense of the revolutionary government. This appointment proved one of the turning points in his career.

By good fortune, when he arrived at Toulon, he found that the general in charge of artillery was one of his former teachers in the Military College. The general had full confidence in his pupil and gave Napoleon a free hand in drawing up plans for driving out the English and vanquishing the Royalists.

Napoleon studied the maps of the city and its fortifications very carefully. It was clear to him in a moment that all depended on the control of the harbor itself. And he recognized that the most important fort to recapture was the one at the end of the long cape. He, therefore, mounted his cannon in strategic places behind the fort and opened fire.

When this key fort finally fell, the English realized that the remaining forts could not be defended and, seeing masses of French troops descending upon the city from the surrounding hills, they quickly embarked and escaped. The Royalists could not hold out alone and once more Toulon became part of the French Republic.

It was at this time that Barras was one of the government representatives in Toulon. He was present during the siege and he saw the young officer Napoleon in action.

When the siege was over, all the military officers at Toulon admitted that the key to the victory lay in the capture of the fort at the tip end of the cape. For this brilliant plan and for his services, Napoleon was commended to the Minister of War.

The Minister of War, sitting in his office in Paris, was

impressed with the reports of the siege and happy that the English had been driven out. He rewarded Napoleon for his part in the recapture of Toulon by promoting him to the rank of general. That is how at the age of twenty-three Napoleon became one of the youngest generals in the French army. A fortunate combination of circumstances had given him a chance to display his rare talents.

But now Napoleon's brilliant career suffered a serious setback. He was sent on a secret mission to Genoa and when he returned to Paris he was accused of treasonable action, and tried by a military court. Although he was acquitted he was transferred from the artillery to the infantry, where he was given a post in the map-drawing department.

He bitterly resented this degradation and he tried desperately to have himself reinstated in the artillery. He even wrote letters to the National Committee of Public Safety in which he described the fine services he had rendered the army. But these letters did not bring the result he desired. Instead he was ordered transferred to the Army in the West. This was even more humiliating than working in the map-drawing department and he did everything he could to delay his departure.

Somehow, month after month, Napoleon managed to put off leaving Paris. He kept hoping that something might happen so that he would not have to join the infantry. And something did happen.

It was just at this time, as good fortune would have

it, that rioting broke out in the streets of Paris against the National Convention and the new Constitution. It was at this time that Barras, now a member of the Convention, was elected Director of Defense and charged with the task of quelling the riots. And it was at this time, in the early hours of the morning, that Barras remembered Napoleon at Toulon and, turning to those beside him, said, "I have just the man we need. He is a little Corsican officer who will not stand upon ceremony."

Then Barras went to his desk and quickly wrote to Napoleon. That morning at ten o'clock he was appointed to defend the city. And in the afternoon his cannon blasted out that famous "whiff of grapeshot" which saved the government from the mobs. He became second-in-command under Barras and in a short time this victorious defender of Paris was made Commander in Chief of the Army of the Interior. He was twenty-six. He was already famous.

*   *   *

As Commander in Chief of the Army of the Interior, Napoleon had the task of defending the government of France from internal disturbances as well as from foreign invasions. He lost no time reorganizing every branch of the service. He at once promoted all those who had worked with him and assisted him, for now that he was the most important military man in all Paris he wanted his fellow officers to share in his success. He bore no grievances against those who had at times opposed him.

He treated all with full generosity, for he was eager to win friendship and loyalty. He had dreams for the future. He had plans, and he knew he would need the support of all the able officers in his army.

While Paris was dancing and celebrating the victory, Napoleon was busy renewing old friendships, meeting people of influence and making new friends. A "whiff of grapeshot" had unexpectedly brought him power and fame. Fate and Fortune seemed to be on his side. And he realized that now the door to the future had swung wide open.

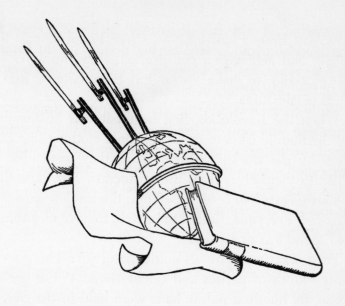

II

THE ROAD TO DESTINY

Paris was dancing. The Revolution was over and the people were happy.

It was now six years since the fall of the Bastille and during this time the streets of Paris had seen much bloodshed. And the guillotine had cut off the heads of thousands of aristocrats as well as the heads of Louis XVI and Marie Antoinette.

The people had had enough of blood and violence.

Now that France had become a free Republic and the people had achieved a constitution, they threw off all restraint and, to make up for lost time, entered into a whirl of pleasures.

When the Revolution first began it was fashionable for the middle class to dress in simple clothing like that worn by the working people. Thus they were able to separate themselves from the aristocrats. But, now that the aristocrats had been wiped out, the fashion suddenly changed; everyone wanted to be rich, to have nice things and spend lots of money.

Paris was swept by an epidemic of joy. There were daily rounds of parties and celebrations. At this period alone, six hundred public balls were held in the city. A dancing fever took hold of the people. But no longer did they like the dignified quadrilles and minuets. The Revolution had even changed the style of dancing. A new kind of whirl, imported from Vienna and called the "waltz," was now the fashion everywhere. All Paris was waltzing.

The Revolution had destroyed the aristocracy of France. But now that it was destroyed the people wanted to enjoy themselves in the manner of aristocrats. They wore elegant clothes and went in for dancing, drinking and gambling. And some of the better educated women, married to government officials, even held salons in imitation of the grand ladies of the old regime. Their homes were frequented by celebrities, actors, artists, writers, speculators who had made money on the Revolution, social climbers and adventurers. Napoleon, eager to meet influential people and make new friends, often visited these homes.

At one of the most famous of these Paris salons, the one presided over by a Madame Tallien, Napoleon met a charming young widow by the name of Josephine de Beauharnais. He fell madly in love with her.

Napoleon at this time was not an impressive figure. He was short, lean, haggard and shy. His skin was pale, with an oily sheen; his cheeks were hollow and his dark hair hung to his shoulders in untidy strands. He stood with a slight stoop, and the coat of his uniform was too long. His shoes were in need of repair. All in all, as he stood in the midst of this brilliant gathering, he seemed out of place. Looking at him, many wondered how such a strange unkempt fellow could have the rank of general and be the Commander of the Army of the Interior.

But if one happened to catch the glance of his serious deep-set eyes, and if one spoke to him, then one quickly understood that he was completely indifferent to outward appearances. He had a magnetic personality.

Josephine de Beauharnais was one of those who spoke to him.

❉   ❉   ❉

Josephine had lost her husband, an aristocrat, during the Revolution. She herself had been imprisoned for a short time in a dungeon and had barely escaped the blade of the guillotine.

She was born in the West Indies on the French island of Martinique, the daughter of a French planter. Here she grew up in a semitropical world of sunshine and happiness.

In her tenth year she was sent to a convent near her home where she learned reading, writing, arithmetic, spelling, music and dancing. After five years her education was over. She came home with a few accomplishments: a beautiful handwriting, an expressive style, a musical voice and, above all, a most agreeable and friendly manner. It was her manner, her charm, that captivated Napoleon.

His manners were crude. He did not always bother to make himself agreeable. His speech was often blunt and lacking in grace and courtesy. All these things, which he lacked, he found in Josephine. It did not matter to him that she was several years older than he and that she had two children by her late husband. From their first meeting, in spite of his shyness, he was determined to marry her.

"I was certainly not insensitive to feminine charms," he said many years later to some of his companions, "but I had never till then been spoiled by women. My character rendered me extremely timid in their company. Madame de Beauharnais was the first woman who gave me any degree of confidence. One day, when I was sitting next to her at table, she began to pay me all manner of compliments on my military qualities. Her praise intoxicated me. From that moment on I confined my conversation to her, and never left her side. I was passionately in love with her, and our friends were aware of this long before I ever dared to say a word about it."

After several months of romance Napoleon and Josephine decided to marry. But the notary, who made out the marriage contract and was one of Josephine's friends, secretly advised her against marrying "an obscure little officer who has nothing besides his uniform and sword and has no future." She should rather cast about for someone of more worth. He thought that with her charm she might attract a wealthy man, perhaps a speculator or army contractor.

Napoleon was in the next room and could hear every word. But he did not disclose what he had overheard, nor did he hold it against the notary. He considered that the notary was advising his client to his best ability. Years later, however, he had his revenge. After his coronation as Emperor, this very same notary appeared before him on a matter of business. Napoleon smiled and observed that Madame de Beauharnais, now that she was Queen of France, had after all done very well to marry that "obscure little officer who possessed nothing besides his uniform and sword and had no future."

"Yes," the notary agreed, "she has done very well."

The day after the notary had drawn up the marriage

contract, Napoleon and Josephine were married in Paris at the registry office in the presence of several friends, including Director Barras. Inside Josephine's wedding ring were engraved the words "To Destiny."

* * *

A few days after their marriage Napoleon was appointed commander of the French army stationed on the Italian border. Like all the other countries of Europe, Austria was against the democratic ideals of the French Revolution and was eager to crush the new regime. She had collected forces in her northern Italian states and was preparing for an attack.

The Directors of the government in Paris ordered Napoleon to destroy this threat even if it meant invading Italy.

At this time the map of Europe looked very different from what it does today. The territory which we know as Germany was then made up of numerous states, each with its own ruler and laws. The Italian peninsula was also divided into separate duchies, kingdoms and states. Most of these were under the political domination of Austria.

The spirit of liberty which motivated the French Revolution had crossed the boundaries of France and spread into the surrounding countries. The kings of these lands were against democratic ideas and were eager to destroy the new regime in France. They aided the Royalists and threatened invasion. France was forced to defend herself. As a result, Belgium and all the German states along the Rhine were annexed to France. When the French armies entered Belgium the people welcomed them as liberators. Holland became a sister Republic, and Spain, although she remained an independent state, became closely allied to France.

Such was the map of Europe when Napoleon was given command of the Southern Army on the Italian border.

The dream of his youth was now before him. Here was his chance to lead an army, to invade, to conquer.

He left Josephine in Paris and started without delay for headquarters in Nice. From reports he knew that he would find these southern troops in a miserable condition. But they were now his troops and he was confident that he could bring to the dejected men a fresh spirit and give them enthusiasm and the will to conquer.

He made his plans during the journey from Paris to Nice. And at every post-station, where his coach stopped for fresh horses, he sent a letter to his charming and idolized Josephine. In these letters he professed his devotion, his loyalty, his love.

And the words "To Destiny," engraved in her wedding ring, he assured her would now be fulfilled. He was on the road.

* * *

Arriving in Nice, he found his troops, which numbered

fifty thousand men, in a most deplorable state. He had expected to find them lacking in clothing, food and other necessities, but he had not expected to find conditions quite so bad. Nor did he expect to find the discipline and morale of his men so very low.

He set to work like a demon. He took command of every situation. No detail was too small to receive his personal attention.

He sent a dispatch to the Directors in Paris. "You are asking me to perform miracles and I cannot do that. . . . Only with prudence and foresight can we achieve great ends. It is but a step from victory to defeat. In affairs of magnitude I have learned that, in the last resort, everything invariably turns upon a trifle."

Every detail, therefore, was to him important. In the first few days of his command he gave his attention to the building of a new road, the suppression of a mutiny in one company, horse stealing, dishonesties among the purchasing officers, food, short weight and a number of other matters.

During the first twenty days of his command he issued one hundred and twenty-three written orders. His presence was felt in every part of his widely scattered army. He brought courage to the disheartened men. He brought them a new hope and a conquering spirit. He told them that he did not intend to keep them on the French border fighting a defensive action. He would lead them in an attack against the enemy into the rich lands of northern

Italy. In battle they would win. They would be conquerors.

The extreme confidence Napoleon felt in himself, he transferred to his troops. He brought a new spirit to the army. Never before had the men felt themselves so close to a commander in chief.

However, Napoleon knew that the enemy was ready to defend northern Italy and he knew that their forces were superior. He also knew that a barrier of mountains separated France from Italy and that from Nice to Genoa the roads along the coast were blocked by the enemy armies of Austria. But he had a plan. He would overcome superior forces with new tactics and military strategy. He knew the value of artillery. Cannon had driven the English from the fort at Toulon. Cannon had stopped the mobs in Paris. And with a surprise attack and cannon he could certainly destroy the enemy's center, then attack the right wing with his full force and finally swing around and destroy the left. By dividing the enemy into three parts he would at every moment be attacking with superior forces.

But, before putting this plan into action, Napoleon knew that he had to win a battle of another sort. He had to win over all the seasoned generals under him. He knew that men who had spent a lifetime in the service might hesitate to follow his lead. He recognized his shortcomings only too well; he was only twenty-six and did not look too impressive. But he was determined that he would be the one to give orders and they would obey. He adopted as his motto "I command or I am silent."

At their very first meeting Napoleon faced the hardened, weather-beaten generals with an air of authority. He questioned them on the position of the men, their supplies, their weapons, their endurance. He discussed with them his plans for invasion and he tactfully sought their opinions and approval. He took them into his confidence, but at all times he maintained his position as their Commander in Chief. The generals at once recognized his brilliance and keen military knowledge. The meeting which Napoleon had feared was now over. He had won.

All, officers and men, fell under the magic spell of his personality. In a very few weeks the army was ready for invasion.

Napoleon called his men before him and told them that they were ready for the attack. In order to penetrate the mountain passes and surprise the enemy from the rear they would have to move in rapid marches. They must, therefore, consider tents, baggage and supply wagons as useless luxuries. They must rely wholly on the land for their food. Victory would not be accomplished except through hardships. Only in this way could they hope to reach the rich lands of Piedmont, Lombardy and Parma.

For hardships he promised them victory; for sacrifice he promised them glory.

"Soldiers," he cried, "you are naked and ill fed; the government owes you much and can give you nothing. The patience and courage you have shown are admirable, but they gain you no renown; no glory results to you from your endurance. It is my intention to lead you into the most fertile plains in the world. Rich provinces and great cities will be in your power; there you will find honor, glory and wealth. . . . Will you be wanting in courage or perseverance?"

The men cheered wildly in reply to their Commander in Chief.

*　　*　　*

Late that night Napoleon started his men on their march across the mountains. In the morning the surprised enemy found the French army at their rear. This quick maneuver not only disorganized the central army of the Austrians but separated them from their allies, the soldiers of the King of Sardinia, who was also ruler of Piedmont.

In the two days that followed, Napoleon's men fought four heavy battles, inflicting serious losses on the enemy. They pressed on and at last they found themselves in the rich, bountiful lands of northern Italy. The men now had plenty of food and loot, just as Napoleon had promised.

Forced marches soon brought the French army into the heart of Piedmont and here, in the capital of this small duchy, Napoleon established his headquarters in the king's palace. The king had fled.

At ten-thirty that night two representatives of the king, high officers, arrived to discuss the terms of peace that had been offered by Napoleon. They were brought into the palace and received by Napoleon's chief of staff. But they did not have long to wait, for very soon Napoleon himself appeared before them. They were surprised at his youthful and casual appearance. They noticed that while he wore a general's uniform and high riding boots he was without sword, hat or scarf. They also noticed that his eyes were reddened from lack of sleep. His face was pale. The fatigue of battle was plainly visible.

But although Napoleon was young and his appearance informal, he received the emissaries with assurance. His greeting and manner clearly showed his self-confidence and sense of superiority.

The officers of the king spoke and Napoleon listened patiently. They said that their king, Victor, was anxious for peace but that he considered Napoleon's terms severe. He asked that they be reduced.

Napoleon drew his watch from his pocket and looked at it. "Gentlemen," he said, "I call your attention to the fact that our next attack is fixed for two o'clock in the morning. Unless my terms are accepted the attack will not be postponed a single moment. It is possible that I may lose battles, but never shall it be said that I lost one moment through overconfidence or neglect!"

His forceful and determined manner made it clear to

38

the king's envoys that the terms could not be altered. No bargaining was possible. Their king could only continue to rule on Napoleon's terms. And Napoleon would broach no delays. The advantage he had gained by victory he would not weaken by compromise.

The treaty was signed at once and sent to Paris by special courier, for approval. This was the very first treaty that the young General Napoleon Bonaparte dictated to a European king. And this first treaty served as a model for many that were to follow.

It was now evident to the government in Paris that this young Commander in Chief of the Army in Italy was not only a military genius, a designer of new war strategies, but also a master statesman.

＊　＊　＊

With Piedmont, the gateway to Italy, in his hands Napoleon marched forward into Lombardy. He called his troops together.

"Soldiers!" he said. "In fourteen days you have fought six battles; you have captured twenty-one standards, fifty-five cannons and several fortresses. You have conquered the richest territories of Piedmont. You have taken fifteen thousand prisoners and killed and wounded ten thousand. . . . When the campaign began, you were destitute of everything; today you have plenty and to spare. You have captured large supplies from your enemies. Siege artillery and field artillery have arrived.

"Soldiers! Your country is entitled to expect great things of you. Will you justify her expectations? Your greatest obstacles are already overcome, but you have many battles still to fight, many towns to capture, many rivers to cross. Is there one among you whose courage fails him? . . . Do you not burn with the ambition to spread the fame of France throughout the world? Is it not the desire of every one of you to humble those proud rulers who would fetter us in chains!"

At the same time he issued a proclamation to the people of Italy. "Peoples of Italy! The French army has come to break your chains! The French are the friends of all peoples! Meet them with confidence! We shall respect your property, your religion and your customs. We wage war as generous-minded foes, and turn ourselves only against the tyrants who seek to enslave us!"

These words were accepted by many of the people in Italy. Although they did not like to see French armies invading and conquering their land, still the spirit of liberty, which set off the Revolution in France, had spread to other parts of Europe. And the Italians hoped that the French armies would now break the political domination which the Austrian Hapsburgs held over them. They reasoned that it was better to be ruled by the French, who believed in the Rights of Man, than by the Hapsburgs, who believed in tyranny.

And so, in the name of Liberty, Napoleon marched forward to conquer.

*　　*　　*

However, the road to victory was dangerous. Napoleon's army was hemmed in between the mountains and the sea. It was a hostile country. But he kept urging his men on. He told them that they were now entering a "promised land" and he assured them glory and riches.

During these days he was constantly with his men, sharing their hardships and working late into the night taking care of every detail. He rode on horseback visiting each company in the ranks. Even the most trifling military matter had his personal attention.

The Austrian armies trying to defend northern Italy were confounded by Napoleon's new type of warfare, which was winning him one battle after the other. They could not understand the secret of his success. It consisted of two simple elements: the spirit to conquer which he inspired in his men and a concentration of strength upon one objective. He said, "The essence of strategy is, with a weaker army, always to have more force at the crucial point than the enemy." And if, as sometimes happened, the enemy had more force than he had at a given point, he would divide this force into two parts and attack each separately.

To carry out these new tactics Napoleon's men had to fight harder and march farther. But they were victorious, and this new type of warfare was soon known as "the Napoleonic touch."

At one time during this first campaign in Italy an old Austrian officer was captured and brought to French headquarters for questioning. He was asked what he thought of the state of war. "Nothing could be worse," he replied, not knowing that Napoleon was present. "Here is a young French commander who knows absolutely nothing of the rules of war. Today he is in our rear, tomorrow on our flank and the next day again in our front. Such violations of the principles of the art of war are intolerable!"

Napoleon changed not only the strategy of war but also the strategy of peace. When Milan fell he levied a tax on the city that approximated four millions dollars. And besides this he took twenty famous paintings by old masters. These he had carefully packed and sent to the Louvre in Paris.

Thus France began to feel the glories of war. Napoleon's victories brought great sums of money to her nearly bankrupt treasury. And great masterpieces of art —paintings, sculpture, tapestries and rare antiques—arrived as trophies to enrich her museums.

At the same time Napoleon took great care that his superiors in the government in Paris should not become jealous of his success. From time to time he sent each official some personal, costly present which he appropriated in Italy. In this way he maintained the full support of the heads of government at home. From every dispute he emerged victorious.

Napoleon's armies fought on through northern Italy, winning victory after victory. And with each new French victory the enemy paid tribute. When the Pope's troops, which had joined the side of Austria, were defeated, the Pope was forced to relinquish certain ancient territories, pay a sum equal to five million dollars and surrender one hundred famous paintings. He himself was allowed to remain in Rome only as nominal master of St. Peter's.

In time the Austrian army was completely beaten and Austrian domination of Italy was shattered. Most of northern Italy became part of the French Republic, and southern Italy came under French influence.

At this great conquest all France rejoiced.

❊　　❊　　❊

Through Napoleon, France now began to enjoy the glory of conquest. But through him she enjoyed a still greater glory! Napoleon had transformed a wretched band of Frenchmen into one of the finest armies in Europe.

Returning to Paris, Napoleon was the idol of the people. He was showered with presents and honors. Even the name of the street on which he lived was changed. It was now called *Rue de la Victoire*. The people could not do enough to honor the young general who had brought glory to France.

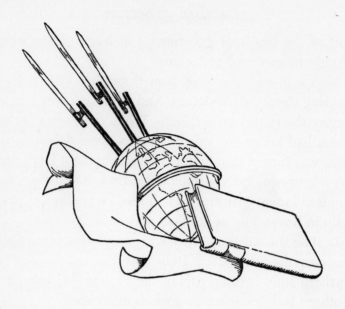

III

THE ADVENTURE IN EGYPT

The government in Paris, encouraged by Napoleon's victory in northern Italy, decided that now was the time to attack another enemy, England. During the Revolution and the years which had followed, England had supported the Royalists of France. She was a bitter enemy of the young democratic government and was, little by little, taking over French possessions in the West Indies. Her strong navy also raided and captured French vessels on the high seas and was strangling the trade routes of France.

The idea of invading England and humbling her had great popular appeal. All classes of Frenchmen volunteered for service in this venture. A wave of enthusiastic recruits filled the army ranks.

But the longer Napoleon worked on plans for the invasion of England the more he realized that such a venture was doomed to failure. The powerful British navy could easily prevent a channel crossing, and an entire French army might be lost in these turbulent waters. He, therefore, presented a counterplan.

In reporting to Talleyrand, the French Minister of Foreign Affairs, Napoleon said: "Europe is but a molehill; all the great glories have come out of Asia." He then went on to explain that, if France were to conquer the island of Malta and the land of Egypt, England would be cut off from her richest possession, India. In time the English would be driven out of India and then the wealth of the Orient would belong to France.

Napoleon was fired with the idea of glory and plunder. And, having rivaled the exploits of Caesar in Italy, he now dreamed of following his footsteps into Egypt. From Egypt he dreamed of going on to Asia, to India. Like Alexander the Great, he saw himself leading a conquering army through the snowy passes of the lofty Himalayas.

Napoleon's plan for the invasion of Egypt was soon

45

approved by the government, and preparations were begun. While England was guarding the channel ports and keeping a sharp lookout for a French invasion from Normandy, Napoleon was secretly gathering an army and ships in southern France. In time he had a force of forty thousand soldiers and four hundred vessels.

He addressed his troops, promising to lead them, in the name of the Goddess of Liberty, to a place across the Mediterranean where glory and fabulous wealth awaited them. He also promised that each soldier, no matter what his rank, would receive seven acres of land. But exactly where this land was located he did not say.

To make certain that he would not miss any valuable works of art and to give his military expedition a high character, Napoleon enlisted the services of one hundred French scholars. These distinguished men were to travel with the army into Egypt, where they would then devote their time to the study of Egyptian history and culture. Egypt was at that time a land shrouded in mystery, for the key to her hieroglyphics had as yet not been discovered. These same French scholars were also to select the finest treasures of Ancient Egypt for shipment back to France.

In time everything was ready, but the French forces could not sail. The harbor of Toulon was blocked by Admiral Nelson and his British men-of-war. And, since Napoleon did not dare to risk a sea battle, he waited, hoping that Nelson and his naval force would be called away on some other mission. By good fortune he did not have to wait very long. A terrible storm came up over the Mediterranean and many of Nelson's vessels were so disabled by the gale that he was forced to seek the harbors of Sardinia, where he could repair the damage.

This was Napoleon's chance. As soon as the storm had blown away, his ships sailed out into the Mediterranean straight for the island of Malta, which he conquered without any difficulty. Then he made for the coast of Egypt.

Egypt, which was then a province of Turkey, was wholly unprepared for an invasion. City after city fell to the French troops.

But while the French conquered cities they were helpless against the nature of this ancient land. They were forced to march over burning sands which reflected the dazzling sun and blinded their eyes. The air was hot and filled with insects of many kinds. The climate sapped their energy. Water was scarce and bad. When a refreshing breeze came, it carried with it a cloud of sand. Vegetables and farm produce did not exist and the food they carried with them from France was soon gone. They were hungry and exhausted.

The soldiers began to grumble. Where were the treasures? Where were the promised seven acres of land? They could see nothing but desert and miserable villages sunk in poverty.

It was only Napoleon's presence and spirit that kept

the men from breaking out into open mutiny. He rode through the ranks and urged them on with visions of victory and glory ahead. He warned his officers against talking sedition. And he forced the men to march on and on until at length they came within sight of the pyramids. Here he found a force of Turkish soldiers blocking the way.

Before the battle began, Napoleon addressed his troops. He called upon them to uphold the honor of France. History would bear witness. "Soldiers," he said, "from the summit of yonder pyramids forty centuries look down upon you."

The French forces formed into squares and awaited the attack. The Turks rushed against the solid lines of bayonets and bravely met French fire. But after several charges their lines grew thinner and their spirit weakened. This was the moment Napoleon was waiting for. He now gave the order for attack.

Confusion and terror followed. The French rushed upon the Turks and drove them into the Nile, where many drowned. Those who managed to save themselves from the water were killed without mercy when they reached the shore.

Now, at last, the French soldiers were rewarded for their sufferings. They rifled the bodies of the slain Turks and, since it was the custom of these men to carry all their wealth on their person, a single corpse often yielded gold and jewels worth a small fortune.

The result of this battle, known today as the Battle of the Pyramids, was the surrender of Cairo and lower Egypt to Napoleon's forces.

And everywhere that the French army went, the one hundred scholars studied the temples, tombs and ancient monuments. They made detailed drawings and records of everything they saw. And they amassed a great store of treasures, from the time of the Pharaohs, which they shipped home to France.

One great contribution to world learning came out of this Egyptian expedition. While Napoleon's scholars were gathering ancient treasures for shipment to France, they came upon an inscribed stone in the town of Rosetta. The inscriptions were in three languages and provided the key to Egyptian hieroglyphics. Through the discovery of the Rosetta Stone and its preservation by Napoleon's scholars, the history and culture of ancient Egypt was revealed to modern man.

The soldiers were satisfied. The scholars were happy. But each night when the men were asleep, Napoleon spread the charts of Asia on the floor of his tent and studied them by candlelight. Egypt was already his. But he dreamed of greater conquests. India was still far away.

*   *   *

While Napoleon was conquering Egypt, Nelson was searching the Mediterranean for the French fleet which had escaped from the harbor of Toulon.

49

One evening, just at dusk, he discovered the French vessels in a port near Alexandria. He did not wait until morning, but with daring seamanship he attacked immediately. He was determined, at any risk, to destroy the French fleet. The battle raged through the night, lighting the harbor with the flames of burning vessels.

When dawn came, only two shattered French ships remained. These managed to escape to the open sea. The rest had all been destroyed or captured. The French flagship had been blown up, killing everyone on board— even the admiral. Thousands of sailors had died; only three thousand managed to survive by swimming to shore.

This naval battle, which destroyed the entire French fleet and which is recorded in history as one of Nelson's greatest victories, cut Napoleon and his men off from their homeland. There could now be no hope of getting fresh troops and supplies from France. They would have to live entirely on what they could forage in Egypt.

But such a disaster did not daunt Napoleon. To make up for this naval defeat he planned victories on land. He marched his troops across the Nile delta and into the Holy Land and Syria. He stormed the ancient city of Jaffa, where in three hours his soldiers killed three thousand Turks and captured another three thousand.

These prisoners, however, presented an awkward problem. Napoleon had barely enough food for his own men. He, therefore, ordered the Turkish prisoners marched to the sandy beach. Here they were divided into small groups and shot. "Necessity," he said later, "left no room for mercy."

The bodies of these unfortunate men were gathered together into a pyramid, and even thirty years later their white bones were seen by passing steamers. This pyramid of bones has been condemned by history. Massacre of defenseless prisoners was even then against the rules of war.

After the capture of Jaffa, Napoleon and his army marched on; but they were no longer successful. The walled cities of the Orient were like fortresses. They were not easily taken and the cost in men killed and wounded was too great. Privations of all kinds began to be felt and the officers and men lost heart. So Napoleon, no longer able to keep up the spirit of his men and fearing mutiny, decided to leave Syria and return to Egypt. But this was not an easy thing to do, for there were many wounded and sick within the ranks. Many had unfortunately contracted the plague.

Some of the wounded could be shipped to Egypt by sea; the rest could be carried on stretchers across the hot desert lands. But those sick with the plague presented a special problem. These men, stricken with an incurable and contagious disease, could not be taken along with the army, neither could they be left behind to the mercy of the enemy. Napoleon, therefore, decided that they should be given an overdose of opium and released from their suffering. This was done and in later years this act, too, Napoleon defended by saying that in such an emergency one has little choice.

But, although he was at times most ruthless, Napoleon showed a genuine concern for his men. And because of this trait he always retained their admiration and love. He was more than their commander; he was one of them. He was their friend. On the march back to Egypt he ordered that all the horses be used for transporting the wounded. And he and his officers walked in the ranks.

The journey was a perilous one; but at length Napoleon brought his men safely back to Egypt, where he at once set to work to establish French rule over the newly conquered territory. Since he did not have ships to carry his army back to France, and since his forces were not in condition for further military conquest, there was nothing else for him to do. He, therefore, put war aside and turned his thoughts to peace.

As governor of Egypt, he drew up plans for the building of roads, irrigation ditches and schools. He ordered the construction of bakeries, breweries, windmills and water mills, powder factories and printing plants. He set his scholars to work on a number of projects. They engaged in research on vegetables dyes, local plants, the fishes of the Nile and epidemic diseases. He sent out explorers to search for minerals. He ordered his scholars to compile an Arabic dictionary. All these works and a hundred more he instituted with great energy.

But his genius went still further. He had the vision to foresee the need of a canal at Suez. Such a canal fitted in with his dream of linking the East with the West. And he ordered his engineers to make soundings and measure the water levels of the Mediterranean and the Red Sea.

Napoleon understood the work of governing and the work of transforming a backward country into a prosperous one. Had he remained in Egypt for some time, he would no doubt have brought a new life to this desolate land. But few of his plans were carried through, for he suddenly returned to France.

*　　*　　*

The situation in France was serious. She was threatened with invasion on every side and her government seemed confused and helpless.

Napoleon, learning of this, secretly decided to turn over his command in Egypt to his generals and return to Paris. He felt that, with the tense situation at home, the French would have forgotten his failures in Egypt and he would be free to take advantage of the political unrest to further himself.

But, before he could set sail for France, an event occurred which was most fortunate for him. A great Turkish force landed on the Nile delta and started marching against his armies. A victory against the Turks at this time would pave his way in Paris. Instead of having to live down past failures, he could return once more as a hero.

Napoleon, therefore, acted without hesitation. He attacked the enemy at once, before they had a chance to receive supplies or reenforcements. His artillery blasted them apart and his cavalry charged the fragments that remained. So sudden and furious was the battle that two thirds of the Turkish force was killed. Those who survived, surrendered.

Napoleon now secretly set sail for France on a merchant ship. It was a long voyage and a dangerous one. For forty-seven days he sailed through the Mediterranean toward the coast of France in constant danger of being captured by the British. But finally he landed safely on French soil and hurried north to Paris.

And, just as he had hoped, the news of his last great victory over the Turks was already known. Once more he was welcomed as a hero. Once more he was the idol of the people.

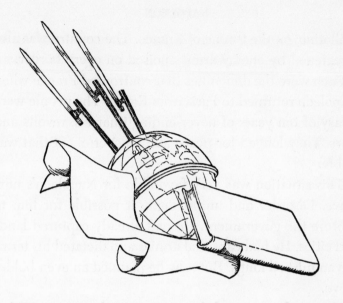

IV

FROM GENERAL TO RULER

The Republic of France, which had been born of the Revolution, was now ten years old. It had weathered a stormy course. The old order had not been put aside without protest and violence. The new order lacked direction, plan and unity. Within the government there were constant quarrels. And against the government there were endless Royalist plots to put the brother of Louis XVI, whose head had fallen under the blade of the guillotine, on the throne of France. The country was also threatened by enemy armies poised on every border.

Such were the difficulties that confronted France when Napoleon returned to Paris from Egypt. The people were weary of ten years of never-ending quarrels, revolts and wars. They longed for peace and a government that was stable.

This situation was very favorable for Napoleon's next move. Disorder and unrest made it possible for him to capture the government. He had already captured lands and cities. He had captured armies and dictated his terms to vanquished kings. But now he planned an even bolder move.

He openly criticized the government by saying, "What have you done for that fair France which I left you so prosperous? For peace I find war; for the wealth of Italy, taxation and misery. Where are the one hundred thousand brave French whom I knew in Italy—where are the companions of my glory? They are dead!"

With the help of his elder brother Joseph, who had entered politics, and of his younger brother Lucien, who had recently been elected president of the lower house of representatives, known as the Council of Five Hundred, Napoleon had himself appointed supreme commander of all troops in Paris, including the National Guard. This appointment was of great importance to his plan.

As soon as he was in command of these troops he declared that a state of emergency existed and that he was ready to defend the government of France.

Then, with his generals, he appeared before the upper chamber, known as the Council of Ancients. And with words of flattery, and insisting that he was acting only to relieve the emergency, he won them over. "You are the wisdom of the nation," he proclaimed. "I come surrounded by the generals of the Republic, to promise you their support. Let us not lose time looking for precedents. . . . Our arms shall be put in execution. I come accompanied by the God of War and the God of Fortune. Let those who love me follow me." These words brought him a cheering vote of confidence.

Now it only remained for him to win over the lower house of representatives, the Council of Five Hundred. However, this task was not to prove quite so easy. Many of its members were ready to resist the dictates of a military leader.

Escorted by his troops, Napoleon rode out of Paris to St. Cloud, where the lower house was in session. But before he entered the hall a heated debate concerning him had already begun. Some insisted that the Constitution must be preserved at all cost. "The Constitution or death!" cried many from the benches. "Down with the dictator!" Lucien Bonaparte, as chairman of this council, had great difficulty maintaining order.

At length the moment came for Napoleon to appear before them. He left his troops in the courtyard and,

taking four strong soldiers to serve as a personal bodyguard, he entered the chamber.

As soon as he appeared, there was a violent outcry
against him. "Outlaw!" cried some. "Traitor!" cried
others. "Down with the tyrant!"

So violent was the feeling against him that some,
shaking their fists, rushed forward to attack him, and
one deputy, from his native island of Corsica, drew a
dagger and waved it aloft. His bodyguard protected him,
but so fierce was the rage against him that he was forced
to back out through the door and seek safety in the hall-
way.

He was completely unnerved by this hostility. As the
hero of France he had not expected this kind of recep-
tion. His face was pale and he was perspiring. He stam-
mered; he became hysterical. He clawed his cheeks with
his fingernails until blood flowed. The iron nerves which
he had displayed on the battlefield were completely
shattered. He could stand up against cannon fire but not
against personal opposition.

As he staggered out into the courtyard, he stam-
mered to his soldiers, "I offered them victory and fame.
And— And they have answered me with daggers." Then,
suddenly, he seemed to recover. He turned to his men
and called out in a loud voice, "I have led you to victory,
to fame, to glory. Can I count on you now?"

"Yes!" came the thundering reply. "*Vive Bonaparte!*"

As these words rang out his brother Lucien, unable to

restore order in the chamber, rushed into the courtyard. He faced the assembled troops and, finding them in a high state of excitement, for they imagined that the blood they saw on Napoleon's face was due to an attack upon him, he cried out, "General Bonaparte, and you, soldiers of France, the President of the Council of Five Hundred announces to you that evil delegates armed with daggers interrupt the deliberations of the council. He authorizes you to employ force. The Council of Five Hundred is dissolved."

Napoleon at once ordered a detachment of his men to enter the hall and end the assembly meeting.

But many inside the chamber refused to leave their places and protested against this armed intrusion. It was then that an officer shouted to the soldiers, "Throw the whole lot of them out. Drag them out by force!" To accomplish this more troops were brought into the hall and many of the elected delegates were carried out bodily.

Napoleon, mounted on horseback, waited in the courtyard. He saw his soldiers drag the elected representatives of the people out of the building. He was silent. He was in command.

Lucien Bonaparte now hurried to the Council of Ancients to announce that the Council of Five Hundred had been dissolved because they had attacked his brother, Napoleon, with daggers and had declared him an outlaw. Lucien then demanded that the Ancients vote at once to place the government in the hands of three men, Consuls, who would rule and carry on the affairs of the state during the emergency. A vote was taken and the motion approved. And Napoleon was appointed one of the three Consuls.

Thus the government by elected representatives of the French people was dissolved in a single day. And in its place a dictatorship was established. In this way ended the government born of the French Revolution.

❊ ❊ ❊

The Council of Three was from the very start dominated by Napoleon's personality. He displayed a remarkable talent for statesmanship and under his influence the Council was surrounded by the best advisers in the land. Talleyrand was retained as foreign minister.

From the very beginning the Council took firm hold of the reins of government. Immediate steps were taken to balance the budget; priests and loyal nobles who had been living in exile were invited to return to France; a reorganization of the army was ordered; a national bank, the Bank of France, was established; a constitution, long overdue, was promised.

When the new Constitution was drawn up, it was Napoleon who announced its democratic virtues to the people. "Citizens! The Constitution is grounded on the true principles of representative government, on the sacred rights of property, of equality, and of liberty."

While this new Constitution maintained many of the civil rights gained by the Revolution and established legislative bodies of elected representatives, namely a Conservative Senate, a Tribunate and a Legislative Senate, it betrayed the true spirit of democracy. It retained the supreme rule of the Three Consuls, and provided that one of them should be a Chief Consul. And through this provision Napoleon became First Consul of France.

His first act as Chief Consul was to move the government to the old Palace of the Tuileries, the palace of the kings of France. Here, only a few years before, in the great open square before the palace, the guillotine of the Revolution had stood. Here Napoleon had seen the gathering mobs and the uneasy King of France wearing the red cap of the Revolution. It was here that he had exclaimed, "Poor driveler! . . . If he had swept away five or six hundred with his cannon, the rest would be running yet."

And now into this same palace, the Tuileries, the home of the kings of France, he moved his wife, Josephine, and her two children. And in this same square he, as head of the French government, reviewed his troops.

      ✵   ✵   ✵

Very soon after Napoleon became First Consul word of Washington's death reached France. When this sad news arrived, Napoleon issued a general order commanding all the flags of France to be draped in crepe for ten days in honor of "a great man who fought against tyranny and consolidated the liberties of his country."

It was the will of the French people to pay homage to those who had fought for liberty, and Napoleon was, at this time, very careful not to oppose public sentiment. He knew that his power depended upon his popularity.

* * *

As First Consul, Napoleon gave his personal attention to every branch of the government. He worked with untiring energy. From chaos he brought order. And uncertainty and fear were soon displaced by a feeling of security. In a short time there was not a person in France who was not aware of his leadership.

But, although Napoleon had established order within France, the country was still surrounded by a ring of threatening enemies: England, Austria, Russia, Turkey, Portugal, Naples and the Vatican in Rome. They refused to recognize Napoleon's new government and called France an aggressor and a threat to the peace of Europe. Had she not recently, under the very leadership of Napoleon, invaded Italy and Egypt? Had she not, a few years back under the Revolutionary Government, invaded Belgium, Holland and the Rhineland? Had she not recently also invaded part of Switzerland? Where would she halt?

To counter this hostility, Napoleon tried to get the enemy nations to come to terms. As ruler of France he considered himself the equal of any ruler in Europe. He, therefore, dictated a letter to the King of England. His message began with the words "Must the war, which for eight years has ravaged the four quarters of the world, be eternal? Is there no room for reconciliation?" And in conclusion he pointed out that "the fate of all civilized nations is concerned in the termination of war." This was a definite plea for peace.

But the English constitution prevented the king from replying personally. His foreign minister, however, wrote to the French foreign minister to say that peace was not possible until the causes of war were removed. This same letter advised Napoleon to restore the exiled royal family to the throne of France.

Napoleon, of course, had no intention of restoring the Bourbon kings of France. Nor would the French people have tolerated such a move.

In fact, when the brother of the beheaded Louis XVI wrote to Napoleon from exile suggesting that he return to France and mount the throne, Napoleon truthfully warned him, "You must not think of appearing in France. You could not do so without marching over five hundred thousand corpses."

It was plain that the kings of Europe did not relish a Republic in France. Power seized through revolution, they considered wrong. Only royal succession did they consider legitimate. The kingdoms of Europe did everything possible to aid the exiled French aristocrats. They supplied them with money and even encouraged them to plot against the government of France.

But all the Royalist plots against France were trifling compared to the constant threats of war and invasion. Because of these threats Napoleon was forced to keep an army in the north to protect the coast from the English and also to guard the Dutch frontier from the intrigues of the House of Orange. He had to hold a second army to watch the Rhine. A third army guarded the Swiss border. And a fourth was in Italy.

This fourth army was in a deplorable condition. It was under attack by the Austrians and was unable to hold the lands which Napoleon had conquered a few years before. It had already suffered several defeats, and the wonderful spirit that Napoleon had once instilled in the men was now broken. The soldiers were in desperate need of supplies; their leadership had failed and the coast of Italy was blockaded by the English fleet. In their distress and disorganization many left the ranks and wandered off on their own. Whole battalions deserted!

France was threatened by invasion on every side. And the most serious threat of all was the one on her Italian border. The near collapse of the French army in northern Italy opened a direct route into France for the Austrian enemy.

* * *

Napoleon drew up plans for a second Italian campaign. He was determined to drive the Austrians out of

Italy once and for all. The campaign which he conceived was as daring and as adventurous as any military enterprise in the history of the world. It also proved to be one of the shortest, for Napoleon devised a way by which he could annihilate a whole enemy army in a single stroke.

Knowing that France was filled with foreign spies watching every movement, Napoleon employed a ruse to cover his plans. He ordered a mobilization of troops close to the German-Swiss border. This was immediately reported abroad by the spies. And the enemy concluded that Napoleon intended to march this army to the relief of his forces in Genoa.

Napoleon, however, had no such intentions. While these troops were gathering, three French columns were secretly marching into Switzerland under the command of trusted generals. They were to converge close to the Great St. Bernard Pass and here await further orders. Even the generals did not know Napoleon's full plans.

On an appointed day Napoleon reviewed the decoy troops gathered on the German-Swiss border. This event was immediately reported to Austria by her spies. And the enemy now felt it was only a matter of days before these troops would start southward. They were in the open. They could be watched. There was plenty of time.

But what the Austrians did not know was that, as soon as the review of the troops was over, Napoleon got into his carriage and ordered his drivers to race toward the

Swiss border. By traveling all night he reached Geneva the next morning; here he was met by several of his trusted generals. They had full reports ready for him on all the wild passes of the Alps.

They reported that the roads were mountain paths, too narrow for wagons and artillery, dangerous for horses and men and blocked in places by great snowdrifts. He was surely not thinking of marching a whole army over such perilous terrain!

But Napoleon was impatient. He did not desire any opinions. He asked quickly, "Is it possible to pass?"

"The thing is barely possible," was the reply.

"Very well," said Napoleon. "Forward! Let us proceed."

*   *   *

Napoleon divided his soldiers and supplies into four separate divisions. In order to diminish risk and gain time, each was ordered to cross the Alps by a separate mountain pass. The most difficult pass of all, Napoleon reserved for himself and the men under his command. He led about half of his entire force, sixty thousand men together with artillery, horses and supplies, over huge barriers of the Great St. Bernard.

He marched his men and rolled his artillery as far as the road permitted. From this point on, everything—men, horses and cannons—had to be moved along the narrow snow-covered ridges of rocky precipices and over dangerous glaciers.

The moving of the cannons presented the greatest problem, and this had Napoleon's personal attention. The guns were dismounted and fitted into logs which had been hollowed out. When each cannon was secured within the tree trunk, ropes were attached and to these ropes the men were harnessed. By sheer strength they dragged these heavy loads. The larger cannons were so heavy that it took a hundred men to move each one of them.

The gun carriages were also taken apart and the wheels removed. Each piece was then carried on poles borne on the men's shoulders. Powder and cannon balls were packed in boxes and strapped to the horses and mules.

Sometimes Napoleon, dressed in a plain gray military coat without any markings of rank, rode on a mule; but more often he walked with the men, cheering on those who had the great burden of dragging the heavy logs which encased the cannons.

At one place high on the mountain Napoleon met a young shepherd and asked him if he would be willing to act as a guide over the icy top, for the wind had blown the snow into drifts which concealed the path. The shepherd lad was quite willing and so he walked beside Napoleon at the head of the troops.

The boy knew every turn of the hidden path and he led them on without hesitation. But there was one thing he did not know; he did not know that he was guiding

Napoleon, the First Consul of France and Commander in Chief of all her armies.

As they walked along, the boy and Napoleon spoke of many things and the boy became very friendly and confessed everything that was in his heart. "You know," he said, "someday I hope to have four hundred sheep grazing on this mountain slope, and then, too, when I am older I hope to be able to buy a plot of land and build a nice house."

"Is that all your heart desires?" asked Napoleon.

"What more could I want? If I had a flock of sheep and a home I would be the happiest man in the world."

When the soldiers had reached the top of the mountain and were safely started on the descent, Napoleon bade farewell to the shepherd boy. He thanked him for everything he had done; then, writing a note on a piece of paper, he handed it to the lad.

"Can you read?" he asked.

"No, sir."

"Well, it does not matter. Take this letter back to the St. Bernard monastery and give it to the French officers stationed there. They will reward you."

The boy delivered the message as he was instructed. And one of the officers asked him, "Do you know what this message says?"

"No, sir. I can't read."

"Well, it says that you are to be rewarded for your services to our Commander in Chief. You will receive, at once, enough gold for four hundred sheep, a fair piece of land and a good house."

The gold coins were counted into a leather pouch while the simple shepherd boy stood by. He looked on with big wondering eyes. He was dumfounded. Never in his life had he seen so much gold. He had dreamed of a fine flock of four hundred sheep and a snug home, but he had never expected that these things would come to him so easily and so suddenly.

An officer held out the bag of gold, but he hesitated to reach for it.

"Take it," said the officer. "It was Napoleon himself that you guided over the mountain."

*   *   *

It took four days for Napoleon's army to cross over the mountain passes of the Alps.

All four forces joined on the warm southern slope. Here they rested while the cannons were taken out of their protective log casings and mounted on the reassembled gun carriages. The horses were put back in harness. And soon the men and artillery were on a good road headed toward the enemy.

Before long the artillery, which Napoleon had brought over the Alps, opened its thunderous fire against the surprised Austrians. Napoleon's troops had suddenly appeared at their rear. They were attacked where they were least able to defend themselves; for their whole artillery was at their front, pressing hard against Genoa.

This position, which Napoleon had achieved through danger and daring, had still a further military advantage. It completely cut off the Austrians from their supplies and their home bases.

The crossing of the Alps by Napoleon's army has been hailed as one of the most brilliant strategies in all military history. The result was the quick and complete devastation of the enemy.

In the battle that followed, the Austrian forces, which numbered more than the French, were completely destroyed.

Through this single victory, known as the Battle of Marengo, France regained everything that she had lost during the preceding year in Italy. And it proved once more that French troops could be victorious if only they were led by Napoleon.

*　　*　　*

Returning to Paris, Napoleon was once more the hero of the day, the idol of France.

It was barely two months since he had left Paris to review the decoy troops on the German-Swiss border. And in this short space of time he had moved a whole army over the Alps and brought them to battle. In this short space of time he had closed the path of an Austrian invasion into France and completely annihilated the enemy.

Paris went wild with joy. Never before had a French hero been acclaimed with such enthusiasm. And Napoleon, feeling that he had the full confidence and love of the people, decided that now was the time to advance himself one step further. Ambition in his heart burned with a hot flame.

Accordingly a close friend presented a resolution in the Conservative Senate. This resolution, which was to mark the gratitude of the people, provided a second term of ten years for the First Consul, to begin when his present term expired. It was immediately passed. Napoleon, however, protested that he would not accept a prolongation of his powers without the consent of the people. The public would have to vote on this resolution.

But when the ballot was prepared, the wording was changed by Napoleon himself. The question which the people were asked to vote upon was "Shall Napoleon Bonaparte become First Consul for life?"

His victory was overwhelming. Over three and a half million people voted "Yes." Only eight thousand voted "No."

And so by popular acclaim Napoleon became First Consul for life. He was now thirty-three years old. Step by step he had risen. But the ambition in him still glowed, for there remained one more step to which he could rise. The crown of France was still before him.

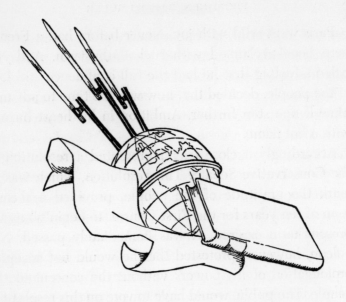

V

FIRST CONSUL

What was the inner character of the man who passionately desired the crown of France? Was he a genius? Was he a demon? He was both.

Napoleon had in him strange contradictions. He was a mixture of good and evil, a mixture of keen intelligence and deep ignorance. He was a man of great charm and offensive rudeness. At times he displayed a wonderful talent for organization, and at other times he was careless and neglectful. He had audacity and because of this he succeeded, he succeeded gloriously; but when he failed he failed miserably.

Napoleon was five feet six and one-half inches tall, which was under average height for a Frenchman at that time. Most of his officers were a good deal taller and for this reason he gained the nickname "Little Corporal." In his youth he was thin and looked sickly. But after his return from Egypt his health was more robust, and during the years that he was First Consul he gained so much weight that he appeared quite stocky.

His strong features were finely chiseled and his eyes were bluish-gray, not black or brown as represented in some paintings. In certain lights they took on a greenish cast, and when he was enraged they became hard and challenging. He had a quick, penetrating glance which took in everything. No detail escaped him.

His voice was rough and not very musical, yet there was great charm to his conversation. This came from the quality of his mind and the direct expressiveness of his language.

His hair was never black as some artists have recorded it, but rather a deep shade of chestnut brown. When he was young he wore it quite long, but after he returned from Egypt he cut it shorter. And when he became First Consul he cropped it.

He liked to dress simply and only on very special occasions did he wear the gold-embroidered uniforms of his rank. In the field he always wore an overcoat of plain dark gray and a black three-cornered hat. He never wore epaulets or other ensignia of rank. His gray coat and three-cornered felt hat were known everywhere.

His amazing energy and vitality enabled him to work day and night. He needed less sleep than most people. And often on campaigns, when weary, he rolled up in his greatcoat and slept for a few minutes on the ground wherever he happened to be. A short nap refreshed him and he was again filled with energy.

Night after night, while on a campaign, he remained awake studying maps, issuing orders and inspecting his outposts.

He often spent the night memorizing the dossiers of those recommended for decoration on the following day. In presenting honors to his men, he always liked to add a personal touch.

The next day he walked along the line and stopped before a young soldier. "You are Paul Mirabeau." The soldier smiled, proud that Napoleon should know him. Napoleon also smiled, and led him forward a pace or two out of the line for all to see. Then he added, "I have been watching you for some time. You were first with our Forty-eighth Regiment, then you were transferred to the Fourteenth. You were with me in Egypt. You helped drag one of our cannons across the Alps. And you were in the first line of fire at Marengo. For distin- guished services I now award you the insigne of the

Legion of Honor." Then, while tucking the red ribbon into the buttonhole of the soldier's coat, he added, "I have learned that your mother has recently been ailing. I hope she is better soon. You are to have a few weeks' leave to go back to your farm and visit her. . . . When you do so, be sure to remember me to the people in your village of Alfort."

Napoleon had memorized all this personal information the night before. And the record of young Paul Mirabeau was not the only one that was clear in his mind; he had also familiarized himself with the records of the other twenty or thirty soldiers who had been recommended for decoration.

When Napoleon was at home, in Paris, he usually got up at seven o'clock in the morning. While his valet shaved and dressed him, he dictated to one of his many secretaries. When he was dressed, he drank a cup of tea and then went into his study. Here he looked over the letters and messages which he had dictated the evening before and which scribes had copied during the night. He never signed a letter or order without reading it over carefully.

When this was done, he and his secretary attacked the pile of mail that was waiting each morning. For this task he seated himself on a sofa before a small round table and slit open the envelopes. He glanced rapidly at the contents, and if the letter required no reply he threw it on the floor. Those that could be answered briefly he passed to his secretary, who marked in the margin the

75

words Napoleon dictated. Those that required longer
answers were divided into two piles, letters that could
be answered at once and letters that had to be deferred
for lack of information.

When his correspondence was finished, Napoleon
turned his attention to the confidential police reports
that were prepared for him daily. From these secret
reports he learned of conditions all over France. They
helped him keep track of political intrigues, the activities
of the Royalists, the arrival and departure of foreigners
and endless other matters. Even private conversations
were recorded. And Napoleon took great pleasure in
reading bits of scandalous gossip which the police, knowing his interest in such things, had gathered especially
for him.

Each morning Napoleon also received reports from
his agents in the conquered territories and enemy countries. In this way he was kept informed of everything
important that was happening in Europe.

At ten o'clock in the morning he was ready for his
breakfast. This was served to him in his study so that
his work would not be interrupted. After breakfast several hours were taken up by the visits of ministers, military officers, state officials and foreign ambassadors. He
was interested in all departments of the government and
he kept in close touch with their problems and their
progress. He studied departmental reports and publica-
tions so that he might be well informed about everything.

Nothing was too insignificant to receive his attention. His head was like a card index. He loved to pore over statistics and tables.

Among the hundreds of things that required his attention were the building of roads, bridges, schools and museums. He ordered the new roads of France to be built wide, as straight as possible, smooth and well graded. He saw them as military avenues. And to protect the troops from the summer sun he ordered chestnut trees planted on both sides. He thought chestnut the best kind of tree for this purpose because it gave good shade, grew easily and provided fine wood for rifle stocks. To this day chestnut trees line the roads of France.

Napoleon labored all day long and far into the night. His terrific energy wore down his ministers and exhausted his many secretaries. He seemed sustained and stimulated by his own inner desires. He was a little man with the energy of a giant.

While Napoleon was extremely well informed on many subjects, he displayed a stubborn ignorance on certain matters. His idea of women's position was very low. He considered them inferior creatures. Speaking of education, he said, "I do not think that we need trouble ourselves with any plan of instruction for young females; they cannot be better brought up than by their mothers. Public education is not suitable for them, because they are never called upon to act in public. Manners are all in all to them, and marriage is all they look to."

Woman's position was not advanced by the Code Napoleon, which he, as First Consul, helped to create. Under these revised laws a wife still did not control her property, and her money remained legally in her husband's hands. Napoleon also held prejudices against labor and the peasant-farmer. And the Code did not advance their position.

He knew how to be most charming and win friends. That is, when he felt so inclined. Socially he was a mixture of charm and rudeness. There were days when his friendliness won over all who came in contact with him. He was naturally complimentary and generous with his friends and gave them costly presents. However, there were times when he was blunt and deliberately insulting to people without the slightest cause. He lost his temper easily and often when he held court he seemed ill at ease. Josephine, on the other hand, was ever the charming hostess and she did everything she could to counteract the rude behavior of her distinguished husband.

Napoleon often kept his dinner guests waiting for several hours before he appeared. Then when all were seated at the table he would begin eating as soon as he was served. Since he was always served first and since he was a rapid eater, he usually finished before any of his guests. When he was finished, all plates were at once removed from the table. As a result, state ministers and foreign diplomats often went hungry at his feasts! They soon learned to eat at home before coming to one of Napoleon's banquets.

Not only was he late for banquets but he was late nearly every evening for dinner. Because of this the cooks in the kitchen were driven frantic. Since they knew that he loved roast chicken, and that when he wanted it he wanted it in a hurry, they always had a chicken or two turning on the spit before the fire. In this way they had his favorite dish ready for him the moment he arrived.

When Napoleon became First Consul he received a salary of half a million francs a year. Another half million came to him as President of the Italian Republic. But in a few years his personal revenues were increased to over sixteen million francs a year, or about three million dollars in American money.

However, the people of France were so devoted to him that they were happy to pay him this small fortune annually. Had he not brought order out of chaos? And on the field of battle had he not brought them victories against their enemies? Had he not brought glory to France?

* * *

The expense of Napoleon's salary drew heavily on the French treasury. An unsuccessful expedition he had sent to reconquer, from the English, the island of Santo Domingo, in the West Indies, had proved very costly. Money was constantly needed to support the large armies of France both at home and abroad. Huge sums were also necessary for Napoleon's extensive program of public works.

79

To add to these difficulties confronting the French treasury, the English navy began a concerted attack against French shipping. They raided two hundred French ships in various parts of the world and took the cargoes valued at fifteen million francs. The British also invaded Egypt, annihilated the French forces of occupation and took over the land. Everything that France had gained from Napoleon's Egyptian campaign was lost. The British even captured the little island of Malta.

Napoleon was furious and once more he began making plans for the invasion of the British Isles.

England was strong on the sea. France was strong on land. The channel between France and England protected the British Isles. Nevertheless Napoleon hoped to bring England to her knees.

However, in order to fight England, Napoleon needed money. And, since his treasury was low, he cast about for a way to raise the necessary sum. Just at this moment, by good fortune, President Jefferson sent Monroe as a special envoy to Napoleon to discuss the possibility of the United States buying Florida and the town of New Orleans from France.

The United States wanted New Orleans for the protection of her shipping on the Mississippi. And she wanted Florida in order to complete her Atlantic coastline.

The French, however, explained to Monroe that Florida had not been ceded to France in the treaty which

Spain had recently made with Napoleon. By this treaty Spain had ceded only the territory of Louisiana, which included the town of New Orleans.

As the conference continued, Monroe was surprised to discover that Napoleon was not interested in selling only the small town of New Orleans but that he wanted to get rid of the whole of the Louisiana Territory.

It was explained to Monroe that while Napoleon had, at first, planned to colonize the Louisiana Territory the pressing war with England now made this impossible. Land in North America was of little use. What Napoleon needed was money.

Monroe promised to pay France fifteen million dollars for the Louisiana Territory, although he had no authority from President Jefferson or from Congress to do such a thing. He had the vision to see the great value this land would have to the United States. And so he seized his chance.

When Monroe and Livingston, the American Ambassador to France, were signing the documents of transfer, they asked to see a map which would show the boundaries of the land.

The French did not have a map, nor did they seem to know the extent of the land.

"Gentlemen," said Talleyrand, the foreign minister, "you have made a bargain; make the best of it."

In this year 1803, neither the French nor Monroe, neither Livingston nor anyone in America, realized the full extent of the Louisiana Territory. Its southern border touched the Gulf of Mexico. It reached north to Canada. And, what is more, it went westward to the Rockies and Oregon.

In this way, by the stroke of a pen and without firing a single shot, the area of the United States was doubled. Louisiana added over eight hundred thousand square miles to our country.

Both Monroe and Livingston knew that they had exceeded their authority, but they felt that under the circumstances they had acted wisely. And on their return to America their action was approved by Congress.

While Napoleon was not completely happy to part with this land in the New World, still he felt it would be folly to try to retain it in the face of an English blockade. Besides, he needed the money. He said, "I would that France should enjoy this unexpected capital, that it may be employed in works beneficial to her marine."

Napoleon also said that the sale of the Louisiana Territory would benefit France by strengthening the power of the United States. Thus England would be provided with a "rival on sea, one that will sooner or later humble her pride." In this he displayed prophetic vision.

* * *

As First Consul, Napoleon rebuilt France.

Roads, canals and public buildings were constructed. A program of public works was undertaken to provide employment for all. Napoleon believed that only a hungry people would revolt against their government; this was a lesson he had learned from the Revolution.

A new police system was instituted, making the land safe for travelers and commerce. Through the establishment of the Bank of France, finance was placed on a solid footing and a free flow of trade brought prosperity to the land.

It was also at this time that the laws of the land were completely revised and given the name Code Napoleon.

Another important measure which was instituted at this same period was the establishment of a national system of education. Before the Revolution the universities and schools of France were controlled by the Church. With the first violence of the Revolution the clergy had scattered and these institutions had closed. During the ten or more years since this had happened the grade schools had reopened, but the schools of higher learning had not. And so, when Napoleon announced that education would now be a national institution and that the universities of France would now be reopened, he received unqualified approval from the public.

Napoleon not only reopened the old universities but also established new ones, such as the Polytechnic School for the study of engineering and science. And he appointed the best and most eminent scholars of France to head the new educational system.

As First Consul, Napoleon also attended to two other

important matters. These were most serious and required long and careful deliberation. The first concerned the exiled aristocracy of France; the second concerned the religion of France. The people felt very strongly on both these subjects and Napoleon had to proceed with great caution in winning them over to his point of view.

The French nobles, who had escaped the blade of the guillotine, were all living in foreign lands. Napoleon thought it wrong for so many fine French families to be in exile; and he saw no reason why they should not return to France, provided of course they had not plotted against the Revolutionary Government and would now take a vow to support the new regime. He, therefore, called the nobles back to France and even promised, where possible, to restore to them the property confiscated by the Revolution. The majority of the French exiles welcomed this order as merciful and just. Many, scattered by the Terror, returned to their homeland and became peaceful and admiring subjects of Napoleon.

The Revolution had also exiled the priests and closed the churches. During the Reign of Terror a number of priests had been killed and many of the churches ransacked. Now, Napoleon felt, the time had come for a reconciliation.

During his youth Napoleon professed little regard for religion; he felt that Church laws conflicted with national laws. Confronted now with the problems of ruling a nation, he felt differently.

"Religion," he said, "is a principle that cannot be eradicated from the heart of man." On another occasion he declared, "No society can exist without morality, and there is no sound morality without religion. Religion alone supplies a strong and durable foundation for the State. A society without religion is like a ship without a compass."

He spoke these words publicly, but he hesitated to act because so many people in France were at this time opposed to religion. Many felt very indignant because the priests and bishops had supported the nobles in their plots and intrigues against the people's fight for a democratic government.

So great was the public hatred for Rome that Napoleon even contemplated establishing the Protestant religion as the religion of France. Since Protestantism was the established religion of England and Germany, he thought it might also serve France. But he soon abandoned this idea; for he secretly dreamed of crowning himself Emperor of France and her conquered lands which were Catholic, and he felt that such a move would need the support of the Pope in Rome.

He, therefore, proceeded very cautiously and allowed time and publicity to build sympathy for his plan. To his friends he said privately, "How can you have a state without religion? Society cannot exist without inequality of fortunes, which cannot endure without religion. When one man is dying of hunger near another who is ill from overeating, he cannot resign himself to this difference unless there is an authority which says, 'God wills it thus. There must be rich and poor in the world. But hereafter and during all eternity the division of things will take place differently.' "

These were his private opinions, but publicly Napoleon repeated that religion was necessary for the morality and security of man.

In time public opinion was won over and Napoleon sent envoys to the Pope, inviting him to reopen the churches of France that had been closed by the Revolution. However, Napoleon imposed two conditions: the French government would nominate all bishops and cardinals as vacancies occurred, and all church officials of France would henceforth swear allegiance to Napoleon's government.

So eager was the Vatican to reestablish the Church in France that the Pope agreed to everything.

*   *   *

To celebrate this pact with Rome, the Cathedral of Notre Dame, which had been closed for over ten years, was reopened and special services were held. Napoleon attended, accompanied by a retinue befitting a monarch.

The ancient ceremonies which had been destroyed by the Revolution were restored. The Archbishop of Aix, who had once preached the coronation sermon of Louis

XVI, officiated; but he now prayed for the health and well-being of Napoleon, the First Consul.

In this manner, after many careful maneuvers, Napoleon brought the Church back to France. And it was not many months after making peace with the Pope that he recommended that his Uncle Fesch be made the Archbishop of Lyons. Napoleon then asked that his uncle be given the cardinal's hat.

Uncle Fesch had once studied for the priesthood but had put religion aside to become an army contractor during the time of Napoleon's first Italian campaign. In a few years he had made a large fortune and, now that he was quite comfortable, he thought it would be very nice if his nephew would recommend him for a position of dignity. This Napoleon did, and the Pope gave Uncle Fesch the red robes and hat of a cardinal to please the French ruler. But Uncle Fesch did not go to Lyons to fill the vacancy, for Napoleon immediately appointed him Ambassador to Rome. He thought it would be gracious to have a cardinal of the Church serve as French Ambassador to Rome.

These two measures—the return of the exiles and the return of the Church—were generally approved by the public. Napoleon had skillfully managed to bring sentiment around to his point of view. In putting through these measures he displayed his skill as a statesman. He accomplished what he desired with patience, tact and diplomacy.

France, which had been so weary of internal strife and foreign wars, was happy in its new-found security and peace even though the price was dictatorship. As First Consul, Napoleon had the full confidence of the people; and they willingly, little by little, surrendered many of the liberties they had fought for and gained by the Revolution. Slowly democracy was displaced.

Napoleon's court in the Palace of the Tuileries became more and more like the court of Louis XVI. Some of the spirit of the old monarchy began to return. A secret police now scrutinized the people. Strict censorship was imposed and those newspapers critical of Napoleon's rule were closed.

But, while civil liberties were destroyed, the concept of the equality of man was preserved. Ability and merit still counted more than birth. Talent and effort were rewarded in this new scheme of things. Many soldiers from the ranks rose to become generals in Napoleon's army. No man in France, no matter how lowly born, could say that it was impossible to rise to power. Was not Napoleon himself once a poor boy, from a foreign land and from an obscure family? And without wealth or station, with little formal education, had he not risen to the very top?

As long as this spirit of equality was maintained the people of France were perfectly happy to have a strong man like Napoleon rule over them.

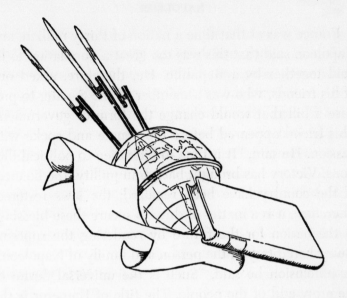

VI

EMPEROR OF FRANCE

Five years had now passed since Napoleon's soldiers had entered the hall of the Council of Five Hundred and dispersed the elected delegates of the people. During these five years Napoleon had served the nation as First Consul. He had proved himself an able statesman and the people were well satisfied with his rule. Now he felt the time had come when he could reach out for the crown of France.

France was at that time a nation of thirty million, and Napoleon said that this was too great a population to be held together by a Republic. He, therefore, asked one of his friends, who was a member of the Senate, to propose a bill that would change the form of government. This friend appeared before the Senate and spoke with passion. He said, "It is time to bid adieu to political illusions. Victory has brought back tranquillity; the finances of the country have been repaired, the laws restored. Therefore, it is a matter of duty to secure these blessings to the nation for the future by rendering the supreme power hereditary in the person and family of Napoleon." In conclusion he said, "Such is the universal desire of the army and of the people. The title of Emperor is the one that best suits the dignity of the nation."

This measure, even though it violated the Constitution, was carried with only one dissenting vote. It was then placed before the people for their approval.

Napoleon, however, having received the approval of the Senate, did not wait for the people to vote. He immediately assumed the dignity and title of Emperor. He gave royal titles to his brothers and sisters and he elevated seventeen of his generals. Some became Marshals of France and some were given titles which had previously been bestowed on the favorite courtiers of the old kings of France. Once again the palace had its Grand Marshal, its Master of the Horse, its Grand Huntsman and its Master of Ceremonies.

Six months later the public voted on the measure. Since Napoleon was already Emperor in practice, the referendum seemed useless and only one-tenth of the people bothered to vote. The result? Three million cast votes in favor of a hereditary Emperor for France, and only twenty-five hundred were opposed.

* * *

Now that France was an Empire, holding the lands of Italy, Belgium, Holland, some Rhinish states and part of Switzerland, and having political influence in Spain, Napoleon thought he would follow the example of his hero, the great French conqueror and emperor, Charlemagne. Like Charlemagne of olden times he, too, would be crowned by the Pope of Rome.

Napoleon was eager to identify himself with this great French hero and carry the minds of the people back to the glories of the past. Now that he was Emperor he did not want the people to dwell on the abuses of the recently dethroned Bourbons. They might begin to draw unpleasant comparisons.

He, therefore, wrote to the Pope asking him to come to Paris to officiate at his coronation. The Pope did not, at first, consent to come, but after Napoleon had written him a second letter he agreed to make the journey.

Elaborate preparations for the coronation were immediately begun. Napoleon was determined that his coronation should be as magnificent as possible. He knew that the public was always deeply impressed by the traditional pageantry of such occasions and he was eager to take advantage of this fact.

The day of the coronation at last arrived and Napoleon and Josephine drove to Notre Dame and in an imperial carriage drawn by eight white horses. In spite of the bad December weather the streets were so crowded that the royal carriage could hardly get through. Because of this the Pope was forced to wait for several hours in the cold unheated cathedral.

At length they arrived and the long traditional coronation ceremony began. It lasted three and a half hours and throughout this time Napoleon's face was stern and thoughtful.

Toward the end of the ceremony, when the Pope raised the crown of France to place it on the new Emperor's head, Napoleon took it from his hands and crowned himself. As it came to rest on his gloomy brow a shout of approval was raised by his friends and intimates who stood nearby. But their acclamation rang with a hollow echo. The vast crowds that filled the cathedral were silent. The brow that wore the crown already felt the weight of uneasy power. But, brushing aside this incident, Napoleon turned to Josephine and placed the Queen's crown on her head.

The little Corsican and the charming daughter of a Martinique planter were now Emperor and Empress of France. He was thirty-five.

The coronation and pageant cost the people of France five million francs. The Emperor's gold crown, made by the court jeweler and modeled after the simple one worn by Charlemagne, cost only eight thousand francs, but the robes of the Empress cost seventy-four thousand francs.

A few months later Napoleon journeyed to Italy, where at a special ceremony in Milan he placed on his head the old iron crown of the Lombard kings. In doing so he repeated the words that had been spoken by the kings of ancient time: "God hath given it me. Beware who touches it!"

* * *

Napoleon's coronation and a great French Empire did not please the other rulers of Europe.

England, Russia and Sweden were the first to join in a league against Napoleon. Their object was to restore independence to Holland and Switzerland, and force French troops out of Germany and Italy. Austria, at first, hesitated to join in this alliance; but when Napoleon crowned himself with the iron crown of the Lombard kings and thus formally annexed lands that had once belonged to Austria, she joined the league against him.

The Czar Alexander now traveled to Berlin to persuade the King of Prussia to join the other nations in their fight against Napoleon. The two sovereigns visited the vault where Frederick the Great was buried, and over his remains they swore solemnly to fight for the liberation of the German states.

France was now encircled by united enemies. War was inevitable.

* * *

Napoleon did not wait for his enemies to gain strength and consolidate their forces for an invasion of France. With his usual daring and courage he took the offensive.

He took half of the army, which had been waiting on the coast of France for an opportunity to cross the channel to attack England, and he marched it across France and the Rhine far into Germany to meet the enemy. This was a bold act but one that again proved his military genius.

So sudden was this move that England, Prussia, Russia, and Sweden had not had time to organize armies in the field. Napoleon, therefore, had only Austria to face.

The French and Austrian forces met just outside of the city of Ulm and a fierce battle ensued, lasting three days. Napoleon displayed amazing military insight, and the result was a complete defeat of the Austrian forces.

The French, now unhindered, marched on toward Vienna, the capital of Austria. The city was not prepared for a siege and surrendered without opposition.

By this time, however, the Russian army had come to the aid of the Austrians. They joined forces north of Vienna, and Napoleon marched forward to engage them in battle. He knew that both emperors were leading their armies, but he also knew that both were inexperienced in military affairs and were certain to blunder. He, therefore, left his plans flexible so that he could take full advantage of their mistakes.

Napoleon did not have long to wait. When he saw the Russian forces move down into the long valley, instead of holding their position on high ground and waiting for reenforcements, he knew that the young Czar Alexander had made his first mistake. "In twenty-four hours," he predicted, "that army will be mine!"

For a few hours that night, Napoleon slept on the ground before a campfire with some of his men. But at two o'clock in the morning he mounted his horse and rode out to inspect his outposts, as was his custom before all battles.

He had hoped that in the dark he would not be recognized, but wherever he went he was greeted by the joyful shouts of his troops. He spoke words of courage to them and told them that he would be watching every move and that if they needed him he would himself come onto the field of battle.

The next morning the sun rose in full brilliance. The French soldiers felt that this was a good omen and predicted victory. But Napoleon knew that victory depended upon strategy and was on the side of the greater cannon.

In the morning, as Napoleon had expected, the Russian generals blundered for a second time. They sent a large division forward to attack the right wing of the French army. This was Napoleon's chance. He quickly sent troops to fill in the gap between the divided Russian forces and cut off their communications; and while the French right wing held out, Napoleon concentrated his fire on the remaining Russian forces. The Austrians tried to come to the aid of the Russians, but Napoleon's artillery, which he had placed on the heights overlooking the battleground, now came into action and poured a rain of shells into their midst.

The emperors of Russia and Austria watched the ruin of their armies from a high hill that overlooked the valley. They issued frantic commands and tried to save some fragments of their forces by ordering a retreat. But it was impossible for them to rally the regiments scattered by Napoleon's artillery.

Never before had Napoleon gained so overwhelming a victory. Of the enemy, there were eight thousand dead; fifteen thousand wounded; and twenty-three thousand prisoners, including eight generals. All the Russian standards and many Austrian flags were captured by the French.

This defeat was a crushing blow for the Czar Alexander. It was only a few years since his father Paul, "the mad Czar of Russia," had been strangled by dissatisfied councilors in a palace plot. The youthful Alexander was very eager to prove to his people and his armies that he was a leader, one who could bring victories and glory to Russia. He was the one who insisted on battle, and he was the one who ordered his generals to attack the French right wing. When he saw the devastating results of his blunders he mounted his horse and fled from the field of battle accompanied by a single aide. The French were in hot pursuit, and it was only by good luck that he escaped capture.

This great French victory is recorded in history as the Battle of Austerlitz, but at the time the soldiers called it the Battle of the Emperors. Never before had three emperors met and fought on a single battlefield.

On the following day the Austrian emperor, Francis, sent a courier asking for an interview with Napoleon. This was granted. When the Austrian emperor arrived he was surprised to find Napoleon's headquarters in an old mill and, seeing his surprise, Napoleon said, "Such are the places you have compelled me to occupy."

"You have made good use of them," replied the Austrian emperor. "They have brought you victories and you have no cause to complain."

During the interview that followed, Napoleon was pleasant and extremely courteous. He agreed to an armistice and he also agreed to allow the Czar to take back to Russia whatever remnants of troops he could gather together.

* * *

At the time of the Battle of Austerlitz, Napoleon was thirty-six years old and had been Emperor only one year.

Through this victory he added more lands to his Empire. The Austrians were forced to surrender their Venetian territories, which Napoleon added to his kingdom of Italy. She also surrendered her ancient possessions in the Tyrol, and several small duchies.

So many lands were now in his possession and so great had been his victories that Napoleon decided to share his good fortune with his family and faithful friends.

He appointed his stepson, Eugene, Viceroy of Italy, and he arranged that the young man should marry the eldest daughter of the King of Sardinia. His brother Joseph he proclaimed King of Naples. On his younger sister Pauline, who had married a prince, he conferred some duchies bordering on Italy. His brother Louis, who had married Josephine's daughter, became King of Holland. By this last act two members of his family were raised to royalty. And General Murat, the son of an innkeeper, who had married Napoleon's younger sister, Caroline, received the title of Prince and Grand Admiral.

But the members of Napoleon's family were not the only ones to be honored; others who had served him faithfully were also rewarded. Talleyrand, his foreign minister, now became Prince of Benevento. General Bernadotte became Prince of Ponte Corvo; and General Berthier, Prince of Neuchatel. His most distinguished marshals were now made dukes, and he filled up the lower steps of the throne with a long list of counts. Everyone close to him was rewarded. He wanted all to share in his success.

Here was a new French aristocracy, one that Napoleon created himself. With these titles went lands, palaces and handsome incomes. Some of the newly created princes drew an annual allowance of a million francs each. In return Napoleon asked only obedience and unqualified approval.

There was one among those close to him who did not give unqualified approval. His old mother did not have confidence in sudden fortune. Most of the money he sent her she saved, saying that a time might come when he would need it. And when he brought her to Fontainebleau, the former palace of Louis XVI, and told her that this was now her new home, she looked about in silence.

"Do you not like it?" he asked. "Is it not good?"

"Yes, it is good," she replied. Then she added, "As long as it lasts."

Somehow his old mother had a feeling that all this sudden glory was only temporary. And she was not wrong.

    *   *   *

While Napoleon was generous and loving to his family and friends, he was severe with others. He ruled with an iron hand and kept a watchful eye on the far-flung lands of his Empire. His police agents and spies were everywhere in Europe.

His conquered lands were under strict military rule. The people had no voice in their government. They were taxed to the very limit and had to supply endless recruits for his armies. Those who had once welcomed the French as liberators now turned against them. The people protested. In Naples riots broke out, but these were soon put down by force.

Writing to his brother Joseph, whom he had made King of Naples, Napoleon sent him the following instructions: "You must shoot down the mobs without mercy; they are too ready with their knives. Only wholesome punishment will strike terror into the Italian populace. At the first outbreak, drive twelve or fifteen thousand of them out of Naples. Naples alone, without Sicily, must bring in about one hundred million in revenue."

Joseph followed his advice, but Napoleon thought he was not strict enough in his rule. He wrote him again. "I am pleased to note that the village of the rebels has been burned. Severe measures are essential. I take it that the soldiers had received previous orders to plunder the village. That is the way to handle peasants who revolt. It is the custom of war, but it is also a duty prescribed by sound policy."

In this manner was Napoleon's strong hand felt everywhere. In Germany a bookseller was arrested for handling a pamphlet which criticized Napoleon. He was immediately tried by a military court, condemned and taken out into the yard and shot. This type of incident was repeated over and over again throughout the French Empire. It was more of his sound policy.

Napoleon's secret police were feared everywhere. No one escaped suspicion. Arrests occurred daily. People were suddenly removed from their families and, without charges being placed against them, were thrown into dungeons. Often they had done nothing more than speak what everyone knew. The prisons of France were soon filled to overflowing, as they had been in the days of the Bourbons before the Revolution.

Year by year censorship of the press grew tighter. No public or private opinion was printed; only official opinion was given circulation, and this opinion was usually a distortion of the truth. Occurrences of public importance were often omitted completely. And so between lies and silence the press degenerated. Many newspapers were closed because they would not comply with Napoleon's wishes, and those that did comply lost their circulation. The public refused to support a controlled press. In time only one or two official newspapers remained in the whole of France.

Napoleon's rule, which had begun with such ardent public approval, now met with disapproval. Unrest and disaffection were secretly eating into the heart of his power, and the people began to wonder if French victories abroad were really worth the loss of freedom at home. The Revolution had been fought to throw off the yoke of a king, and now the people were weighted down by a yoke of their own making. Many wondered if they had not surrendered their freedoms too easily.

Napoleon was well aware of the growing dissatisfaction, and the method which he now used to stem it was the one he had successfully used before: victories and glory for France. He was certain that new conquests would fill the heart of every Frenchman with pride, and he felt that pride was an antidote to the poison of unrest.

He, therefore, began to work on new military plans.

* * *

As he studied the map of Europe his eye fell on Prussia. Here was a menacing military power which should be destroyed. The sooner the better, for had not the King of Prussia sworn a pact against him with the Czar of Russia at the tomb of Frederick the Great?

The forces of the Czar had been annihilated at Austerlitz. Napoleon reasoned that, if he attacked Prussia at once, the Czar would be unable to aid his ally. Ever conscious of the value of time and surprise attack, Napoleon immediately sent his armies across the Rhine—marching toward Prussia.

A few days later Napoleon once again put on his plain gray military coat and three-cornered hat and left the Tuileries. He rode day and night and in time joined his troops far within Germany.

In the meantime the King of Prussia and his court in Berlin had heard of Napoleon's intentions. The whole land became inflamed against the French. While they enjoyed conquering others, they did not like the idea of being conquered. Their land was holy. And they at once advanced to meet the enemy.

In a fever of patriotism their beautiful Queen Louisa

put on her military uniform and rode out at the head of the regiment that bore her name. Young Prussian nobles drew their sabers and sharpened them on the steps of the French embassy.

Napoleon, learning that the Prussians were advancing into the heart of Saxony, knew that battle was close at hand. The advance forces of both armies finally met near the city of Jena.

Napoleon studied the situation very carefully before drawing up his plans of battle. As usual he searched for some weakness in the enemy forces. He found that the Prussian line was overextended and that the concentration of their supplies was not behind the center. Although his main army had not yet arrived he resolved to attack at once with his advance forces. He planned to throw the weight of his attack on the extreme right and seize the stores and magazines, but he knew that this maneuver had to be accomplished quickly before the main body of the Prussian army, a few miles away, could reach the battlefield.

Napoleon, therefore, ordered three whole divisions to move against the objective. In a single battle the Prussian right wing was shattered and the army stores were captured. From this moment on, the main Prussian forces were cut off from their supplies.

The King of Prussia, understanding the great danger of his position, tried to force a passage through the French lines in order to recapture his stores. At this point in the battle the Prussian forces outnumbered the French forces because Napoleon's main troops and heavy artillery had still not arrived. They were some distance off and could not possibly reach the field in time for the battle that was quickly forming and would break at dawn.

But Napoleon was a master of strategy and in the battle that was fought the next day the Prussian army was split into many isolated groups.

On the first day, twenty thousand Prussians were killed and three hundred guns, twenty generals, sixty battle flags and thousands of troops were captured. In the days that followed, the slaughter of the Prussians continued and the isolated groups were rounded up. The Prince of Württemberg surrendered an army of sixteen thousand. The Prince of Hohenlohe surrendered twenty thousand, all that remained of his army of fifty thousand. General Blücher tried to fight on but lost four thousand prisoners besides those killed and wounded. And the King of Prussia fled for safety to Königsberg.

So ended the great Prussian army of one hundred and fifty thousand that had been mustered against Napoleon. In a few short weeks the proud and arrogant Prussian monarchy, built on military power, was humbled.

❊　　❊　　❊

Napoleon and his victorious army went on to Berlin. He entered the city as a conqueror and moved into the palace of the vanquished king.

During the four weeks he remained in Berlin, Napoleon frequently visited the rooms once occupied by Frederick the Great, whom he very much admired. In fact, he admired him so much that he sent his sword and some of his medals and flags back to France. These he counted as rightful spoils of war.

Napoleon also ordered the bronze chariot and horses removed from the top of the Brandenburg Gate and sent to Paris, together with one hundred and sixteen fine paintings and numerous pieces of sculpture. He wanted the people at home to have concrete evidence of his victory.

In the treaty with the King of Prussia, Napoleon took a large part of Prussian territory—all the lands west of the Elbe. He also demanded an indemnity of one hundred million francs.

The Prussians never forgot the humiliation of this defeat. They who loved conquests and worshiped military caste were now forced to bow to a victor. And they had never dreamed that they might themselves be defeated! With Napoleon's conquest their hearts became embittered, and burned for vengeance against the French with a flame that a whole century and a half has not been able to extinguish.

*　*　*

Although the King of Prussia ratified the treaty with Napoleon, he courageously decided to fight on. He gathered together what remnants of his forces he could find and marched eastward to join the Czar, who was now able to aid him with a newly organized army.

Angered at the defiance of the Prussian king and against the advice of his marshals, Napoleon sent his unprepared armies into Poland to engage the Prussian and Russian forces. At the same time he sent home to France for more provisions and men. He also ordered a new conscription of eighty thousand men for the coming year.

The glories and wealth that came to France from Napoleon's victories did not come without the sacrifice of human life. There was hardly a home in France that had not lost a father, brother or son. Some families had lost several members. This drain of life was now seriously felt and the people began to wonder about the price they were required to pay for glory. Fearing to speak openly, they brooded in silence.

But the Senate, under the complete domination of the Emperor, disregarded the temper of the people and at once approved the new conscription.

* * *

The Polish campaign lasted all winter. Many battles were fought, and had it not been for Napoleon's genius and the mistakes of his enemies the French forces would have been annihilated. Even so, Napoleon's armies were very hard-pressed and whatever victories they won were costly and doubtful.

In one battle alone, sixty thousand Russians faced

ninety thousand Frenchmen. After fourteen hours of fierce fighting, neither side had gained a victory and the battleground was covered with corpses half of which were French. But a short time after this, in the Battle of Friedland, Napoleon was victorious, although the victory cost him twelve thousand dead.

The Battle of Friedland was the last battle of the Polish campaign, and an armistice was called. Napoleon, the Emperor of Russia and the Prussian king, with their advisers and statesmen, met at Tilsit to make peace.

Napoleon's conquests were recognized and the Prussian king agreed to surrender forever a section of West Prussia, all his lands west of the Elbe and his holdings in Poland. Prussia was also to pay a further indemnity to France.

The Czar Alexander, on the other hand, made out very well; he and Napoleon became good friends. During the campaign which had just ended, the young Czar had developed an admiration for Napoleon's astonishing ability and was glad to meet him. At the same time Napoleon was flattered that the Czar, a true emperor of royal blood, should treat him as an equal. Napoleon had been Emperor for three years and this was the first time he had been accepted by a European sovereign.

He and the Czar became such good friends that they decided to divide Europe between themselves. In order to do this they felt that they had to meet in great secrecy. Therefore Napoleon ordered his engineers to build a raft in the middle of the Niemen River. Here, in a blue and white tent, the two emperors met. They were completely alone and could freely discuss their ambitions and dreams.

The Czar wanted Russia to expand eastward through Siberia into Asia. Napoleon confided to him his secret dream of conquering England's jewel, India. Together they planned to conquer and divide Turkey. Alone, the Czar would take Finland away from Sweden. To this Napoleon had no objection; after all, Finland bordered too close to the Russian capital, St. Petersburg. The Czar was very pleased that Napoleon was so understanding about this and, in return, he offered no objections to Napoleon's plan to invade Spain and Portugal. He also promised to cut off all trade with Napoleon's enemy, England.

In this way, in a blue and white tent on a raft in the middle of a river, Napoleon and the Czar of Russia privately settled the destiny of the nations of Europe.

They felt they had a perfect right to do this because they considered that Europe belonged to them. "What is Europe?" asked the Czar. "We are Europe."

The two emperors were well pleased with themselves and they promised to meet again.

*　*　*

Through this secret arrangement Napoleon gained a powerful friend. Because of his alliance with the Czar he felt that no one, not even England, would dare to threaten his Empire, which covered a great part of Europe.

He returned to Paris and, filled with a sense of power, dissolved the Senate; he needed no help in ruling from delegates elected by the people. This move wiped out the last trace of democratic government in France.

Napoleon was now a monarch with absolute power. He had reached the height of his career.

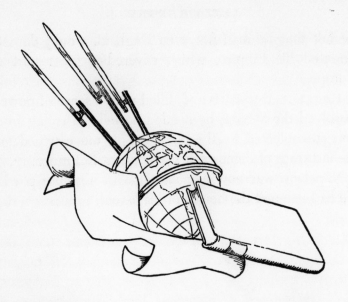

VII

THE PATH DOWN

From the moment Napoleon became absolute monarch of the French Empire, his world began to crumble. As if by some strange stroke of fate, all over Europe the name Napoleon lost its magic.

He was no longer looked upon as the man of the hour. The masses, who had once loved him and believed in him as the leader who would further the ideals of the Revolution, now recognized him as nothing more than

110

another king—and of kings they had had their fill. As soon as he lost the confidence of the people, the rulers of Europe lost their fear of him. Thenceforth they felt that it was only a matter of time before his adventurous course would be ended.

At this time marked changes also appeared in Napoleon's nature. He became impatient and intolerant of everything. He wanted his own way in all matters, and looked upon himself as the appointed master of the world.

Since his coronation Napoleon's relations with the Vatican had become unfriendly. He claimed that he was heir of Charlemagne and, therefore, Roman Emperor. The Pope refused to recognize him. "Your Majesty is doubtless immensely powerful; nevertheless you are chosen, crowned, consecrated and acknowledged Emperor of the French, and not Emperor of Rome."

In order to force recognition from the Pope, Napoleon used threats. He made all kinds of demands and even said that he would divide the Papal States unless the Pope closed his harbors to English trade. When the Pope rejected his demands, Napoleon ordered his troops to occupy Rome.

The Pope remained in the Vatican protected by his Swiss Guard, and retaliated by excommunicating Napoleon.

Such defiance did not please the Emperor and soon thereafter, on the pretext that the Pope's life was in danger, Napoleon placed him under arrest and ordered him brought across the Alps, first to Grenoble and then to the palace in Fontainebleau.

Here the Pope was treated with the greatest respect. He lived in luxury and was surrounded by his own court of cardinals. But in spite of all this he was a prisoner.

The Pope's arrest was only a symptom of Napoleon's new sense of infallibility. He now entered into three other undertakings which were to prove the greatest blunders of his career: he invaded Spain and Portugal; he divorced his beloved Josephine; he quarreled with the Czar and launched an invasion of Russia.

❋   ❋   ❋

While the Czar with Napoleon's consent was taking Finland from Sweden, Napoleon with the Czar's permission launched his campaign against Spain and Portugal.

After fomenting trouble between Spain and Portugal, Napoleon, under the pretext of bringing order to Portugal, received permission from Spain to march his troops through her land. This he did, conquering Portugal with no difficulty and forcing the government and the royal family to flee to Brazil. Spain was pleased. Then Napoleon, taking advantage of his good relations with the Spanish government, advanced his secret plot for the conquest of Spain. To gain this end he resorted to treachery.

He again asked Spain for permission to move troops

across her land into Portugal. He said he wanted to re-enforce his army of occupation, but when permission was granted, he poured an invading army across the French border. So sudden and overpowering was this attack that Spain could offer no resistance and the royal family was forced to flee, leaving Madrid in the hands of the French.

But the capture of Madrid was only a temporary victory. Napoleon had expected that the people of Spain would welcome him—as he had been welcomed in other parts of Europe—as a liberator, or that they would at least bow respectfully before him as did the people in conquered Germany. But to his surprise he found that the Spanish people were different; they were unconquerable.

His French troops won victories, but his soldiers were continually subjected to guerrilla warfare. The public rose up in mobs and killed many of his officers and men. French civilian residents in Spanish cities were slaughtered without mercy.

Napoleon tried to win over the people by instituting political reforms. He issued edicts abolishing the Inquisition, all feudal rights, and regulating the powers of the clergy. But he found that reforms were not welcome, and that the pride and spirit of the Spanish people would tolerate no foreign liberator. In every town and city of Spain the flame of patriotism burned to scorch the conquerors.

So intense was the hatred the French encountered that

Napoleon, for fear of assassination, did not dare to appear publicly in any Spanish city. Of the eleven million people of Spain every one was an open enemy.

Napoleon was determined to make himself master of Spain. He forced the royal family to abdicate and appointed his brother Joseph as King of Spain and Portugal.

When the people heard this they rose in a state of patriotic fury and, surrounding a French army, forced it to surrender. This unbelievable incident gave courage to the British, who immediately, under Wellington, drove the French out of Portugal and, crossing the border into Spain, joined the Spanish patriots in their fight against Napoleon.

This was the beginning of a long campaign in Spain. Napoleon, however, did not stay to lead his troops. He turned his command over to his generals and returned to Paris. He could not understand the hostility of the Spanish people and was eager to get back to France, where he was admired.

*　　*　　*

Napoleon blundered in Spain and, returning to Paris, he made still another fatal mistake.

For many years he had passionately longed for a son, an heir who could inherit his Empire and continue the dynasty he had founded. Since Josephine had been unable to bear him any children, he decided to divorce her and marry again.

Josephine loved him and when she heard of his intentions she was brokenhearted. Nevertheless she accepted her fate and left the court. In the years that followed she remained completely devoted to Napoleon and helped him many times during the dark days which came upon him.

During the long years of their marriage Josephine had shared Napoleon's troubled times as well as his glory. In many ways she had helped him to rise to power. Through her natural charm and grace she had won the hearts of many who proved helpful to Napoleon's career. The people of France and the court were devoted to her.

Yet all this did not prevent Napoleon from casting her aside. The ambition in him was stronger than love and loyalty.

Napoleon decided that his new Empress should be some highborn princess, the daughter of a powerful ruler. Since the Czar of Russia was now his friend, he asked for the hand of one of his sisters. But the Czar would not consider any such arrangement, for, while he admired Napoleon's genius, he did not consider him worthy of a Russian princess of his own royal blood.

Napoleon felt the insult of this refusal which very soon proved to be the wedge that split their friendship.

Having been rejected by the royal house of Russia, Napoleon now asked for the hand of Marie Louise, daughter of his enemy the Austrian emperor. Emperor Francis, unlike the Czar, was delighted to consent to this marriage. He felt that having Napoleon as a son-in-law would prove politically advantageous to Austria. The young Archduchess, twenty-two years younger than Napoleon, was not too eager but was willing to set aside her personal feelings for "the country's welfare."

*　*　*

Marie Louise, a Hapsburg, was pretty, modest and shy. She was well educated and spoke five languages. But her modesty and education did not make her acceptable to the French people.

Marie Louise was a grandniece of Marie Antoinette and for this reason alone many in France disapproved of the marriage. They had not forgotten the indifference Marie Antoinette had shown to their suffering. They felt that her attitude was summed up in a remark she had made when told that the people were clamoring for bread and had none. "Then let them eat cake," she had answered.

Others disapproved because they felt that Napoleon's Empire was purely French and a product of the Revolution and they did not want to see the throne shared with a foreign royal house. Even the Church was against the marriage, and the cardinals of France openly voiced their opposition.

Napoleon, however, brushed all these objections aside and he and Marie Louise were married in the Cathedral of Notre Dame. The ceremony was one of great splendor, and Napoleon's uncle, Cardinal Fesch, presided.

During the ceremony Napoleon looked about. Everything was as he had wished it except that sixteen cardinals were missing from their appointed places, thirteen of them without excuse. The very next day the thirteen cardinals were removed from office and exiled to various remote towns of France. And it was not until Napoleon lost his power, three years later, that these "Black Cardinals" returned to their positions.

*　　*　　*

A year after Napoleon married the Hapsburg princess, it was officially announced that they were expecting the birth of a child. If the child was a girl, she would be greeted with a twenty-one-gun salute; but a son, an heir to Napoleon's Empire, would be greeted with a hundred-gun salute.

And so, early one morning in Paris, when the people heard the cannon start booming they began to count. They counted up to twenty-one, and when the cannon fired the twenty-second shot they knew it would not stop until it reached one hundred.

A son had been born! Napoleon had achieved his heart's desire. And he at once gave the infant the title of King of Rome.

The thousands who had gathered before the palace, on this morning when the cannon began to boom, broke into cheers. "Long live the Emperor! Long live the King of Rome!"

Napoleon's Empire was at last provided with an heir. But would the little King of Rome ever inherit Napoleon's throne, for was not the Empire already showing signs of disintegration?

❖   ❖   ❖

The war in Spain was still on. Wellington and the Spanish people were slowly pushing Napoleon's forces northward toward the French border. His soldiers were so hard-pressed that many of them deserted.

The Empire was also being threatened in other places. Napoleon's friend the Czar, after conquering Finland, cast aside the secret agreements they had made on the raft at Tilsit and was making plans of his own. He wanted to annex more Polish territory and he was preparing for an invasion of Turkey. Napoleon protested, for had not the Czar promised that they would invade Turkey together? Was not Turkey the steppingstone to India? If the Czar should conquer it alone, Napoleon's road to India might be blocked forever.

The Czar had also broken his word with Napoleon regarding trade with England. Russia was exchanging wheat, corn, cattle, hemp and timber with England, in return for cotton and woolen goods, machinery, hardware, boots, china and hundreds of other manufactured goods. This trade destroyed the boycott Napoleon had hoped to impose on England. It was giving comfort and support to his enemy.

And, besides all this, Napoleon had not forgotten how the Czar had insulted him by refusing to give him his sister in marriage.

These were the things that shattered the friendship between the two emperors. Now they were enemies. And to this Napoleon had only one answer—War.

＊　　＊　　＊

In the months before the fateful campaign against Russia, Napoleon began to undergo marked physical changes. Although he was only forty-three he seemed worn out by his tremendous labors. He now avoided exercise and grew fat. He took long hot baths and he often seemed sleepy and tired. The energy which was characteristic of his former years had now left him. He no longer gave his personal attention to hundreds of details. He even became neglectful of important things. For instance, he knew that he should go to Spain and reorganize the army. He alone was capable of doing this, yet he avoided undertaking the task. He delegated this responsibility to others because he knew it would be a long and hard job that would wear him down with fatigue.

Yet, in the heat of his anger against the Czar, he was spurred into action. He planned to march an army across Europe and teach Russia a lesson by crushing her, then march on over the great Himalayas and stab England in the back by conquering India.

Only his body was weary: his passionate ambition was tireless.

Napoleon felt he could accomplish this because he had the greatest army the world had ever seen: all told, he had a million men, recruited from all parts of his Empire. If a million men were not enough to crush Russia and England, he could conscript as many more as he needed. He felt that his supply of man power was unlimited.

With Russia and England at his feet, then Europe would be completely his; and he pictured himself as Emperor of a united federation of European states. "There will be one code," he said, "one court of appeals and one coinage for all Europe. The states of Europe will be melted into one nation, and Paris will be its capital."

And so it was that, with dreams of further glories and full confidence, Napoleon entered upon the Russian campaign without first settling his affairs in Spain. For this reason France was forced to fight two wars at one time—wars in distant lands; lands separated by the whole breadth of Europe. Each war was a blunder. Together they marked his doom.

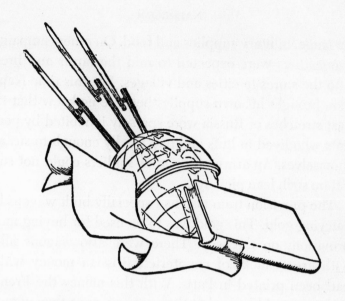

VIII

THE RUSSIAN CAMPAIGN

In the spring of 1812 Napoleon started an army of six hundred thousand troops across Europe toward Russia. He felt that these troops would be sufficient for his projected campaign. He planned to reach Moscow by August, consolidate his gains and then go on to Asia. In his baggage was packed a folding cot with mosquito netting which he would use during the hot nights in India.

With his army there traveled a vast provision train of

121

baggage, military supplies and food. On other campaigns the soldiers were expected to raid the farms and break into the stores in cities and villages. But this time Napoleon brought his own supplies because he knew that the vast stretches of Russia were sparsely inhabited by peasants who lived in huts and had hardly enough to sustain themselves. An army of vigorous soldiers could not subsist on such lean pickings.

The provision train also had specially built wagons for carrying gold. This gold was to be used for buying more provisions on the way. There were also wagons filled with great stacks of counterfeit Russian money which had been printed in Paris. With this money the French soldiers would buy what they needed, once they were in the Czar's domain. This long, heavily laden provision train required thousands of horses to drag it across Europe.

In time the army crossed the Russian border. After this, numerous minor battles were fought with advance Russian outposts. These skirmishes, rain and muddy roads slowed down Napoleon's advances; but in spite of these annoyances, each day the troops drew nearer and nearer to Moscow. However, Napoleon now knew he could not reach Moscow by August.

As they pressed on, meeting only light resistance from the Russians, they traveled through a deserted land. They came upon one empty village after another; villages silent as death, with nothing remaining—neither people nor livestock or food. The peasants had taken everything they owned and disappeared. Where had they gone?

And where were the Czar's armies? Day after day the French advanced and, strangely enough, they met hardly any resistance. Why did the Russians not come out and fight? Was the Czar going to surrender without a battle? These questions Napoleon asked himself as he rode with his troops toward Moscow. At first this strange situation was puzzling; then it became disturbing. Was this a new kind of war? No, surely, he reasoned, when his armies reached Moscow the Czar would meet them in battle.

But Napoleon's reasoning proved wrong. His armies entered Moscow without opposition. The Czar did not try to defend this ancient city. In the face of the invading enemy he drew his armies and the peasants, with their cattle and goods, back farther and farther into the vast interior of his land. He had no intentions of fighting the French at that time because he was waiting for a powerful ally to come to his aid, an ally stronger than any other—Winter.

* * *

Napoleon and his troops did not enter Moscow until the middle of September. He had expected a delegation of city officials to meet him at the city gates, but none was there. He passed into the city to find it deserted. Only a handful of people remained; the rest had fled.

Napoleon had also expected to find Moscow a large

thriving city like those in Europe, one that could house and feed his army of soldiers. But here again he was mistaken. For in this year 1812 the city of Moscow, besides public buildings, contained only nine thousand houses, of which seven thousand were built of logs, and most of the streets were unpaved and muddy. This was hardly a suitable place to garrison an entire army, but Napoleon decided to make the best of it.

He and his staff moved into the Kremlin, the medieval palace of the old Czars. He set to work at once and dictated his terms of peace to the Czar Alexander. This document was entrusted to a Russian nobleman whom the French had captured a few days before. He was liberated on his promise to deliver it to Alexander. Once the peace terms had been sent on their way, Napoleon planned to rest. But there was trouble in Moscow. The city was on fire.

It seemed that when the people of Moscow learned that the French troops were only a day or two from the city gates, they began leaving. And many, not wishing to see their possessions fall into enemy hands, set fire to their homes. Merchants also set fire to their warehouses. Thus it was that, by the time Napoleon's troops arrived, parts of Moscow were already in flames.

The soldiers tried to put out the fires, but the water pipes were broken; the fire apparatus had been removed, the pumps destroyed and even the buckets rendered useless. Besides, the fires were in different parts of the city.

The next night a brisk wind spread the fires still farther. When the flames came toward the Kremlin, Napoleon was forced to leave the city and seek shelter in a suburb.

The fires raged for four days and during this time most of Moscow was destroyed. Only twenty-five hundred houses remained.

At the end of four days Napoleon returned to a city of ashes and charred remains. Once more he took up his residence in the Kremlin. Here he waited for a reply from the Russian emperor.

He waited day after day, but no reply arrived. And while waiting he diverted himself by reading French novels and dictating long reports to be sent back to Paris.

In the meantime his troops were short of food and lodging. There were not enough houses left in Moscow to give them shelter. October was approaching and the nights were growing very cold. The men did not have warm clothing, for Napoleon, having planned to go on to warmer lands in Asia, had not provided for winter uniforms.

The food brought across Europe had now been exhausted and the few peasants still living on the farms outside the city did not bring their provisions into Moscow. Although they were promised good prices and fair treatment, they were afraid and unwilling to help the enemy.

The hungry soldiers began to ransack the city in search of food. They searched every house and all the ruins. They found silks, laces, gold, silver and other valuables. They found stores of wine and liquor, but they did not find what they were looking for and in the end they were forced to shoot their horses in order to survive.

Day after day Napoleon waited for something to happen. He expected a letter of peace from the Czar. Or, failing this, he expected the Czar to rally his Russian troops and try to recapture Moscow. But the Czar did neither of these things.

At one time Napoleon considered pursuing Alexander and forcing him into battle. But he abandoned this idea because he was unable to locate the position of the Russian troops and because he now realized that he was in a trap. The Russians had cunningly retreated before him, drawing him farther and farther into their hostile, barren land. To pursue Alexander would mean going deeper into Russia, farther into the trap.

The month that Napoleon spent in the Kremlin was perhaps the most uncomfortable month in his entire career. He was a man of action. He had marched his great army into the heart of Russia, occupied the ancient capital, and now he was forced to sit and wait.

And as he waited snow began to fall. The nights became colder. Delay was beginning to wear down his victory. Disillusionment was destroying his confidence. His long march to India had now come to a sudden halt.

After the first heavy snow in the middle of October, Napoleon decided that he must begin a retreat. He had still not heard from the Czar.

History can find no parallel to this strange military situation. Here was the most brilliant military genius of his day, a commander who with over half a million men had successfully invaded an enemy land and occupied its ancient capital. He was victorious, yet he was defeated. Because the Russians refused to engage in battle, he and his army were forced to start upon a long retreat—a retreat he had never planned upon.

The tragic march home began on October 19, 1812. Napoleon, unwilling to admit failure, sent a dispatch back to Paris saying, "Moscow is not a good military position. It is necessary for the army to breathe on a wider space."

The army was glad to leave Moscow. It started out in good order, with long files of troops and wagons. The same wagons that came laden with food were now filled with plunder: furniture, Oriental carpets, cases of brandy, libraries of books with fine bindings, silks, brocades, laces, silver, jars of preserves, bags of coffee and hundreds of other precious things. The men were happy with their loot. They dreamed of home.

But very few ever returned to France. Thousands upon

thousands died within the next few weeks in one of the most tragic military debacles in all history.

* * *

To add to Napoleon's misfortune, winter that year set in early. The snow that had fallen while the French were in Moscow was only the silent announcement of something that was to come, something quite overpowering.

As the army slowly retreated, snow began to fall—blanketing the countryside and roads with drifts so deep that the horses were unable to pull the heavy wagons filled with plunder. The men took as much of the loot as they could carry, and many cut up the carpets and made themselves crude overcoats to help keep warm. They plodded on day after day helping the horses drag the cannons and military supplies, and the treasure wagons with gold coins. But, before long, biting winds and zero weather enveloped them. The roads became icy and the horses, not provided with spiked shoes, had difficulty continuing. Many fell and had to be shot.

The land was bleak, barren. Only occasionally did they find a house or hamlet which was occupied. They robbed these peasants of everything they could find—even women's clothing, which many of the men were forced to wear in order to keep warm.

These peasants, whose homes had been robbed, formed into bands which harried the retreating army.

They hunted down the helpless French soldiers and shot and murdered whatever stragglers they found.

To add to these misfortunes, detachments of Russian troops now appeared on every side. Cossack bands swooped down upon them unexpectedly, slashing and ripping their ranks apart. Those who survived fled in terror, leaving their wounded comrades behind to die.

In a very short time Napoleon's grand army disintegrated into pitiful bands of wandering men hopelessly plowing their way through great snowdrifts and over icebound lands.

Abandoning their cannon and throwing away their guns, they trudged on. At this point they were even forced to abandon the treasure wagons filled with gold coins. The men were told to take what they could and they filled their pockets. But the gold did not keep them warm, nor in this wasteland could they exchange it for a crust of bread.

At night groups of men built a great fire and gathered around to warm themselves. In their weariness they fell asleep and by dawn they were often frozen corpses. The heat of the fire melted the snow and, when the fire died out, the zero weather froze the water in which the sleeping men were lying. In this way small groups of men perished. Those who survived were attacked by snipers at the break of day.

By this time the army was so demoralized that every trace of discipline vanished. Each man struggled to save his own life. The horses were shot for food. The wounded and sick, dying helplessly by the roadside, were stripped by their companions of their tattered clothing and worn boots.

All this time Napoleon, brooding and crushed by defeat, traveled with his men. He who had won some of the most brilliant victories ever recorded, now suffered the most devastating military failure in all history. His failure lay exposed before him. On every side he saw misery, ruin and death.

And now bad news reached him from Paris. Rumors of the Russian catastrophe were sweeping France in spite of strict censorship. Napoleon was being openly criticized. In one Paris garrison the soldiers were led to mutiny by their general, who claimed that, since Napoleon was completely defeated in Russia, it was necessary to depose him and establish a new government.

When this news reached Napoleon, he deserted his troops and, with only one companion, made a dash for Paris. They started off in a sleigh taken from some Russian estate. Later, in Poland, where the roads permitted they changed to saddle horses. And finally, close to France, they rode in a carriage.

This dash across Europe, Napoleon and his companion accomplished in the record time of eleven days! He arrived in Paris in time to quell the mutiny and once more secure his position as Emperor.

Behind him in the snows and ice of Russia he had left

the remains of his grand army. He had deserted his men. But in spite of everything they forged ahead with desperate tenacity. Each in his heart hoped that somehow he would manage to get back home to France.

But, of the entire army of six hundred thousand men, only one hundred thousand were fortunate enough to return to France. They straggled back, across the entire breadth of Europe, singly or in small groups, walking skeletons, their clothes in tatters and their feet wrapped in rags. They were living records of an unspeakable horror.

One third of the French army had been taken prisoners by the Russians, including forty-eight generals. The rest were killed or died of hunger and cold.

Up to that time the world had not seen so great a military defeat. The Czar's ally, Winter, had proved more devastating than any army on a battlefield.

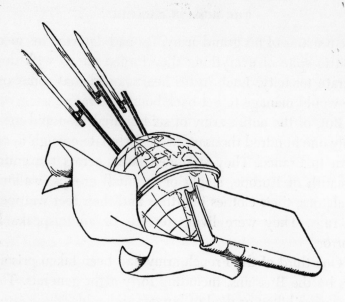

IX

A RING OF ENEMIES

The true facts of the Russian disaster slowly became known in France. The great army was no more. There was scarcely a family that was not in mourning. And among the sorrowing people there arose suspicion and resentment.

Still Napoleon received little public criticism. The magic of his name was such that many rejoiced that he, at least, had returned safely. And officials flocked to the throne to congratulate him and express confidence in his leadership.

However, the people's doubts about Napoleon were soon dispelled by threats of invasion. The kings of Europe decided that now was the opportune time to destroy Napoleon. Having lost his whole army in Russia, he would be too weak to offer resistance. The Czar and the King of Prussia were the first to combine against him. They were joined by Holland, Sweden, England and Austria, forming a solid ring of enemies around France. But before these nations had completed their plans and organized their armies, Napoleon was once more ready for war.

At the threat of invasion France was swept by a fever of patriotism. Once more Napoleon became the hope and defender of the people. They responded to his appeal for a fresh army. Factories worked overtime making guns, cannon and supplies. Everyone rallied to the defense of the homeland. And in a few weeks Napoleon was again able to take the field at the head of a force of three hundred and fifty thousand men. Of this number, however, a great many were untrained and half were under twenty years of age.

* * *

It was at this time that the Emperor of Austria tried to take advantage of Napoleon's desperate situation in order to gain certain territories. He offered to support France against Russia and Prussia if his son-in-law, Napoleon, would surrender the German states and allow the French border to end at the Rhine. If, however, his son-in-law refused to do this, the Austrian emperor threatened to join his forces with those of the allies. He wanted Austria to be the dominant empire of Europe, not France or Russia. And to gain power he was ready to turn against his own daughter, Marie Louise, and her husband, Napoleon.

With the Austrian army on his side Napoleon would have been stronger than his enemies. Nevertheless, to these threatening demands, he sent a sharp reply; he would not surrender one inch of conquered territory. He would not be intimidated. He had fought alone before and would fight alone again.

And so it was that the Austrian army, headed by his father-in-law, joined the forces against him.

✱　✱　✱

Napoleon did not wait for the allies to bring the war into France. He always preferred having the battlefield on foreign soil. He, therefore, marched his army westward into Germany to engage the forces of his enemies: Russia, Austria, Prussia and Sweden.

The first battle in this campaign took place in the spring of 1813. The second and third battles were fought in August, and the fourth battle was fought in the middle of October. This last and decisive battle, fought at Leipzig, is known as the Battle of the Nations. It lasted for three days and it was here that Napoleon met a crushing defeat from which he was never able to recover.

His defense was obstinate and his men fought heroically, but against the superior forces of his enemies his military genius was of no avail. During the first day of battle he lost so many men that at night, in desperation, he sent a personal courier across the battle lines with a message to his father-in-law, the Emperor of Austria. He offered to renounce his rights to Poland and Holland, to evacuate the German states and to grant independence to Italy if the Emperor would abandon his allies and come to his rescue.

But this plea for help was never answered. The emperors and kings who had joined their forces against him had solemnly sworn that they would not deal with him separately. Their strength was in their unity. They would make no treaty with him as long as French soldiers remained on the eastern side of the Rhine.

The battle was resumed in the morning, and again Napoleon lost great numbers of men. Regiments that he had conscripted in Saxony deserted and went over to the enemy side.

On the third day the allies were further reenforced by the arrival of fresh troops. Against such overwhelming numbers Napoleon was helpless, and when he saw confusion breaking out among his troops he ordered a retreat.

He rode on horseback through the battlefield, picking his way over the dead and wounded and around shattered cannon and ammunition wagons. His face was pale. His spirit was crushed. In three days he had lost fifty thousand men. What he saw before him now reminded him of another disastrous defeat, the retreat from Moscow. It was exactly one year, to the day, since he and his troops had started home from the ancient capital of Russia.

The news of Napoleon's crushing defeat at Leipzig spread across Europe setting loose a wave of liberation. Revolts against the French broke out at once in Holland and Italy. New spirit swelled the hearts of the British fighting in Spain. Napoleon's Empire was crumbling.

The allied armies which had fought him at Leipzig now followed his retreating forces toward the border of France. When they reached the border they did not stop; they followed him to the very gates of Paris.

But even with the enemy descending on Paris, Napoleon still hoped to turn the tide. How many times before had he snatched a victory out of defeat? How many times had he won against superior forces by sheer audacity and fearlessness? How many times had he forced emperors and kings to bow in submission? He would do it again!

He conscripted more young soldiers in a last-minute attempt to defend the capital of France. But it was too late. In the city the booming of enemy cannon could already be heard, and the next day enemy troops marched down the long boulevards and the city was forced to surrender.

This was the first time in four hundred years that Paris had been occupied by an enemy.

*   *   *

With the surrender of Paris, Napoleon retired to the palace in Fontainebleau a few miles outside the city. It was to this palace he had once proudly brought his mother. And it was here that she had remarked, "It is very nice as long as it lasts."

It was in this palace that for the last three years the Pope had been held prisoner. Now the allies had freed him. It was here that Louis XVI and Marie Antoinette had lived. It was here he now waited alone. The Empress, Marie Louise, and the little King of Rome, whom he loved so dearly, had been put by the victors, under the protection of the Emperor of Austria. A short time later they were sent to Vienna, and Napoleon never saw his son again.

In Fontainebleau, Napoleon awaited his fate. But he did not wait silently. He addressed a letter to the Czar saying that he was "ready to descend from the throne, to quit France and even to relinquish my life for the good of my country." He offered this sacrifice provided his son, the young King of Rome, were allowed to retain his rights to the throne.

Once again Napoleon received no reply. The conquerors drew up their own terms. They were now dictating; and they demanded unconditional surrender, including complete abdication.

However, the conquerors were not entirely pitiless. Napoleon's life was to be spared and he was to be exiled to the Island of Elba off the coast of Italy, not far from his native Corsica. In the future he was to be known as the Prince of Elba and he was to rule this small island. He was to command a guard of eight hundred men as well as a few naval vessels, sufficient to defend Elba. He was furthermore to receive from the French government a sum of six million francs annually, and the numerous members of his family were to be provided with substantial incomes. The terms also provided that France was to have a new ruler, a royal one. The brother of the beheaded Louis XVI was to mount the throne.

While the victors considered these terms reasonable, Napoleon looked upon them with bitterness. He who was absolute ruler of a vast Empire—an Empire that he himself had made, an Empire which stretched from one end of Europe to the other—was now reduced to ruling an island only twenty miles in length.

All night long Napoleon postponed the signing of the document. He hoped against hope that some miracle would change his fortune. But fortune was no longer on his side. Toward morning, tortured and weighed down by his humiliation, he attempted suicide. But the poison he drank was ineffectual and he was revived by his aides.

Then in the morning, worn out and feverish, he took a pen and scrawled his name to the document which took away everything he had achieved in his lifetime.

* * *

The new sovereign of France, chosen by the kings of Europe, was Louis XVIII, the brother of the beheaded Louis XVI. He was advanced in years and infirm, but to the kings of Europe this did not matter because he was a Bourbon. He was stupid. But they overlooked this also. He was fat and gross, and had vile table manners; but he was of royal blood. And the kings of Europe were determined to wipe out all traces of the democracy born of the Revolution and to restore legitimate royalty to France.

Less than one tenth of the people of France wanted to see the return of a Bourbon to the throne. But this was the choice of the conquerors, and the people were forced to accept the new King without a protest.

On the day Louis XVIII entered the Palace of the Tuileries a cartoonist in one of the Paris papers pictured him as a fat pig. This idea caught the public imagination and, from that moment on, Louis XVIII was nicknamed "Louis the Pig."

* * *

With Napoleon overthrown and a Bourbon king on the throne of France, the victors announced that a peace conference would be held in Austria. All the emperors, kings, princes and rulers of Europe, together with their statesmen, were invited to attend the Congress of Vienna.

Here they were to settle all European disputes. They were to establish boundaries, tariffs, river rights, and to solve a hundred other problems. Here in Vienna they were to remodel Europe and bring peace forevermore.

A few months later, when they assembled in Vienna, each ruler had secret plans; each had studied the map of Europe and was determined to establish boundaries and regulations for his own advantage. Greed came before peace.

Month after month the Congress continued. The map of Europe was cut up a dozen different ways on a dozen different occasions. Some agreements were reached, but not many. The rulers continued to argue and haggle.

There was one point, however, on which all were agreed: the concept of the Divine Right of Kings was to be restored. Blue blood was to be the legitimate ruler of mankind. The aristocracy of birth was to be restored to what it was in the days before the Revolution.

The French Revolution had shaken the very foundation of European aristocracy. The caste system had been overturned by the sudden rise of the common man. But all this was in the past. It was now twenty-five years since the Revolution, and the hateful memory of this time they were eager to erase.

The aristocrats, gathered in Vienna, were determined to forget everything, learn nothing and return to past days. They worked hard to turn back the hands of the clock.

All winter long the Congress was in session. And when spring came, the end was still not in sight.

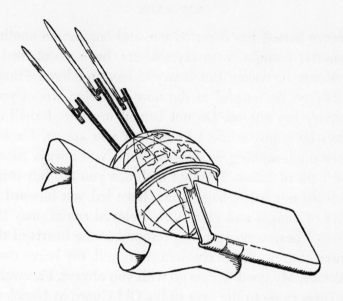

X

THE PRINCE OF ELBA

Napoleon's journey into exile was not an easy one.

On the day he left Fontainebleau for Elba he found his Old Guard assembled in the courtyard waiting to bid him farewell. These were his companions of many battles, companions of many years.

Seeing them, he was deeply moved and he spoke to them. He spoke from his heart.

"All Europe," said Napoleon, "has armed against me.

France herself has deserted me, and has chosen another dynasty. I might, with my soldiers, have maintained a civil war for years. But it would have rendered France unhappy. Be faithful to the new sovereign whom your country has chosen. Do not lament my fate. I shall always be happy while I know that you are so. I could have died, nothing was easier, but I will always follow the path of honor. I cannot embrace you all, but bring forward our battle flags which have led you forward in days of danger and glory. . . . 'Beloved eagles, may the kisses I bestow on you long resound in the hearts of the brave.' Farewell, my children. Farewell, my brave companions. My good wishes go with you always. Farewell."

Tears came to the eyes of his Old Guard as Napoleon quickly turned and entered his waiting carriage to begin the long overland journey to the south of France, where he would then embark for the island of exile.

On this journey Napoleon was accompanied by four commissioners from the four great enemy countries: England, Russia, Prussia and Austria. But he also had with him some of his loyal generals, some friends and a few faithful servants. His retinue filled fourteen carriages. And behind the carriages marched the troops of his Imperial Guard. All these people had volunteered to go into exile with him.

During the early part of the trip Napoleon was welcomed in all the towns through which he passed, but as his procession came into the provinces of the south the sentiment changed. The people were against him and, wherever he appeared, they came out into the streets to jeer. The resentment was so strong and ugly that on several occasions the crowds even threatened personal violence.

This sudden change in public temper was a great shock to Napoleon. Through the years he had become accustomed to wild, cheering crowds. His ears were attuned to the cry of "Long live the Emperor!" Now he found himself regarded with contempt. It upset him and filled him with fear.

At length, to avoid further unpleasantness, he disguised himself by wearing an Austrian uniform. And it was in this disguise that he finally arrived at a small port near Cannes in southern France. He was greatly relieved to find that he and his party were to sail on an English ship, not a French one; for the hostility of the last few days had unnerved him.

As soon as the vessel set sail, Napoleon felt more at ease; and during the days that followed, while at sea, he made friends with the captain and his officers. He even praised the character of the English and made a good impression on the crew. Before the voyage was over, he ordered two hundred napoleons to be distributed among the sailors. Their spokesman came forward to thank him. Removing his hat, the sailor said, "We wish His Honor long life, and better luck next time."

Napoleon was pleased to hear these words and he

143

thought the English crew showed good sportsmanship. It was true his luck had run out, and perhaps next time things might be better. But would he ever have another chance?

It was with these thoughts still in mind that a day or two later he saw the coastline of his island of exile.

* * *

The vessel reached Porto Ferrais, Elba, in the evening. And, fearing that the inhabitants of the island might also be hostile and resent his presence, Napoleon once more disguised himself and, with a trusted companion, went ashore to find out the true sentiment of the people. With his companion he visited the taverns and cafés of the port. He was pleased to find that the people of Elba were ready to welcome him. All felt that his residence would give importance to the island, increase its trade and bring prosperity. Late that night, satisfied and reassured, he returned to the British vessel.

The following morning, Napoleon put on his uniform and made his first public appearance in Elba. The people and town officials welcomed him with all possible respect.

In the first few weeks he established four homes in four different parts of the island. He kept up all the etiquette of the palace in France; and to help occupy his time, he reviewed his troops regularly. He also dictated letters to friends and received news from Europe almost daily. But these tasks were hardly enough to fill his time. He was restless.

One day, while inspecting his island, he climbed a high hill. It was a clear day and from this height he could see the mainland of Italy across the dividing straits. From here he could also survey the entire coastline of Elba, which was perhaps no more than sixty miles in circumference. "It must be confessed," he said, smiling, "that my little island is very small."

But, while Napoleon's island was small, his dreams and his hopes were large. They stretched out over the surrounding waters to the mainland of Europe. He was secretly thinking of escape.

In the months that followed, Napoleon began to make his plans. He carefully read the French newspapers which were regularly sent to him. He watched for indications of unrest in France and he did not have to look far. It was clear from the daily reports in the press that the people were displeased with the Bourbon king who had been foisted on them. They also felt their political humiliation and disgrace. They bitterly resented the rule imposed by their conquerors. Napoleon knew that such unrest and dissatisfaction favored his return.

He furthered his plans by establishing contact with old friends. Many letters were exchanged. Before long his sister Pauline came to visit him. She was a polished master of political intrigue, and he encouraged her to make many trips to Italy. She returned to Elba bringing visitors; old faces and new faces.

Little by little, week after week, Napoleon's plans for escape continued to develop.

Many of his loyal friends had left Paris and were now living in Grenoble, whose main industry was glovemaking. From this city his friends sent him gloves in the fingers of which he found secret messages written on tissue.

"The violets will bloom in the spring," became the slogan of all those in France who were loyal to Napoleon. It meant that in the spring Napoleon would return and once more lead them. And to show their loyalty many wore a little violet ribbon in their lapels.

As the winter months wore on, some of the islanders also began to wear violet ribbons. Napoleon encouraged many of his Imperial Guard to take leaves of absence and visit their homes in France. Furloughs were granted to two hundred of his devoted guardsmen. Each came back to Elba wearing a violet ribbon.

All this was done quite openly, before the very eyes of the British commissioner who was stationed on the island to watch Napoleon's movements; but neither he nor the King of France knew anything of Napoleon's plot. And the other rulers of Europe were much too busy at the Congress of Vienna to bother with what was going on at Elba. They were much too busy bargaining and plotting.

And so it happened that, at the end of February, Napoleon put his plan into action.

One day the British commissioner, who found life on the island very boring, left for a brief visit to Italy. That very night one of Napoleon's larger vessels, which was in the harbor, was quickly painted to resemble a British ship. A hundred men with a hundred paintbrushes soon transformed it. Six smaller vessels were also disguised.

That same night Napoleon's sister Pauline gave a ball to which all the French officers were invited. At midnight the drums in the barracks woke up the men. They were marched out into the dark and were soon aboard the waiting ships. Before long they were joined by their officers, and at the break of day the anchors were weighed and they set sail for the coast of France.

Napoleon, their Emperor, was with them. He had spent ten months on the island of Elba. Now his exile was over.

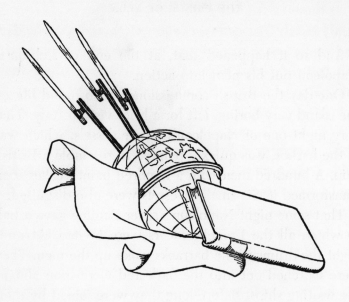

XI

THE MARCH TO PARIS

A few days later, on the First of March in the fateful year of 1815, Napoleon and his men secretly landed on a deserted beach in southern France.

His force consisted of only five hundred soldiers, two hundred dragoons and one hundred lancers. They had with them a few small cannons, but they had no horses. The lancers carried their saddles on their backs.

Napoleon watched his men as they gathered on the

sandy beach. The sun was setting. It would soon be dark and under cover of night he would lead them forward. But first they must eat and rest. He looked about for a safe place to make a temporary camp. Not far away he saw an olive grove. This was a good place.

Fires were soon built and, as the men were resting and eating, a field laborer happened along. Seeing the soldiers, he was curious and drew near. He at once recognized Napoleon and rushed forward with joy.

"Sire! Sire!" he cried.

Then, looking about, he quickly recognized what was happening and he begged to join the soldiers. "I served under you in Italy," he said, and went on to name all the battles in which he had taken part. "And if you will have me," he added, "I am ready to follow you again."

"Here is our first recruit," said Napoleon, turning to his men. He was pleased and considered this a good omen.

The darkness of night was now over them and he ordered the march to begin.

*   *   *

In his march to Paris, Napoleon was anxious to avoid those southern provinces where he had met such hostility some months before. He, therefore, planned to lead his men north to Grenoble on a long hard road close to the Alps. This road led through a countryside that, many years before, had been very active in the Revolution. He felt that if the people of these districts had not liked

149

Louis XVI they certainly must not like his brother Louis XVIII. The years could not have erased their hatred of the Bourbons, and they would, therefore, be friendly to him. Then, once in Grenoble, he would join with his friends.

Napoleon was right. Day after day, as he led his men along the rough, muddy roads through the foothills of the Alps, the people welcomed him. The news of his return to France spread before him, and as he and his men passed through the hamlets and villages the inhabitants came out to cheer them.

Many of the local men joined his ranks. They marched along with his soldiers dressed in their workclothes and without guns or other military equipment. But they marched with spirit, the same spirit that Napoleon had always instilled in them.

In time Napoleon and his band arrived at a town where some of the King's troops were garrisoned, and it was here that he issued his first proclamation. He had had leaflets printed while he was on shipboard during his trip from Elba. The words of the proclamation were stirring.

"Soldiers!" it said. "We have not been beaten. We have only been betrayed. In my exile I have heard your voice. I have arrived once more among you, despite all obstacles and all perils. . . . Who dares pretend to be master over us? Take again the eagles which you followed at Ulm, at Austerlitz, at Jena. Come and range yourselves under the banners of your old chief. Victory shall march again. The national flags will fly again from steeple to steeple and on the towers of Notre Dame. In your old age, surrounded and honored by your fellow citizens, you shall be heard with respect when you recount your high deeds. You shall then say with pride, 'I was one of that great army which entered within the walls of Vienna; which took Rome, and Berlin and Madrid and Moscow; which delivered Paris from the stain brought upon it by treason and the occupation of strangers.' "

Hearing these words read to them by their officers, the soldiers of the garrison felt the pulse of history. And a few minutes later, when Napoleon dramatically appeared before them, they cried out again and again, "Long live the Emperor! Long live the Emperor!"

And the entire garrison joined Napoleon's band of men.

* * *

It was during these first days that the news of Napoleon's landing reached Paris.

The King and his advisers were so stunned that they did not know what to do. Talleyrand, who was now serving Louis XVIII as foreign minister, was in Vienna attending the peace conference and there was no one in Paris who could decide on a course of action. So fast riders were sent to Vienna with the news, and while awaiting orders the very strictest censorship of the press was imposed. Not a word about Napoleon was to be printed.

But wild rumors of the daring landing in southern

France were sweeping the country, and within the next few days the government had to admit the news publicly. But, while admitting that Napoleon and a small force had landed, the government proclaimed him "an enemy of the state and an outlaw." He was to be arrested at once.

On the following day the Paris newspapers announced that the government was safe; the "outlaw" had been abandoned by his followers and was wandering in despair among the hills. It would now be only a matter of time before he would be arrested and made prisoner.

Such were the reports printed in the government-controlled press, but not a word of this was true. Napoleon's victorious march was continuing. Village after village acclaimed him and he was now approaching Grenoble.

Before the gates of Grenoble a whole regiment of soldiers awaited Napoleon with orders to take him prisoner. Soon the men saw their old commander, in the distance, coming fearlessly toward them.

When Napoleon approached he called, "Soldiers of the Fifth Regiment! Do you recognize me?"

At this an officer shouted, "There he is! Fire!"

But before anyone could stir, Napoleon opened his overcoat and cried, "If there is among you a soldier who desires to kill his general, his Emperor, let him do it now. Here I am!"

With one voice the regiment replied, "Long live the Emperor!"

At this Napoleon rushed forward and mingled with the men. He greeted his old companions. Turning to one who was decorated with many medals and had a heavy beard, he said, "Speak honestly, Old Mustache. Would you have had the heart to shoot your Emperor?"

The old soldier drew the ramrod from his gunstock and plunged it down the barrel of his gun. "See," he said. "Judge for yourself. Not one of our guns is loaded. What harm could we have done?"

In this manner Napoleon made his way northward from one place to another, from one garrison to the next. And exactly one week after he had landed on the deserted sandy beach, on the very day that the Paris papers announced that he had been abandoned by his followers and was wandering alone in the hills—on this very day he was leading a spirited force toward Paris. His ranks now numbered seven thousand.

*　*　*

When the news of Napoleon's progress reached Paris, many Royalists flocked to the throne to reassure the fat, worried King.

They said that the whole business was but a political incident and would soon be over. Some called Napoleon an adventurer. Others spoke of him as a "public enemy." And all agreed that he was a "conspirator and outlaw." In this way did they comfort themselves and the King. But not one suggested a plan of action.

153

*　　*　　*

Napoleon marched on. He now reached the large manufacturing city of Lyons. Here, too, the garrison came out to meet him. And here, too, the soldiers joined their old commander. The people of Lyons also welcomed him.

He stayed in Lyons, the second largest city in France, for three days. While his men rested, Napoleon consolidated his forces and issued a proclamation to the people of France notifying them that their Emperor was once more in command.

Then, with complete disregard for the Bourbon King and the Paris government, he published a series of decrees: he ordered that justice be administered in his name, that the chambers of peers and deputies be abolished, and he set a date for electors to come to Paris to frame a new constitution. He also restored the authority of the courts that had been dissolved by the Royalists.

These decrees were immensely popular with the people, and the news of them spread quickly. Even with the strictest censorship it was not possible to prevent this news from reaching Paris. When it did, everyone knew that Napoleon was not wandering through the hills and that he had not been arrested.

*　　*　　*

The King had still not heard from Vienna and he and his advisers did not know what to do.

It was at this moment that Marshal Ney, who had risen in the ranks under Napoleon, came before the throne and volunteered his services. He was in command of a large body of troops which he proposed to march against Napoleon. "In one week," he said, "I will bring Bonaparte to Your Majesty's feet. I will bring him in a cage, like a wild beast."

The King did not hesitate to accept this assistance, and Marshal Ney, kissing the King's hand, started out on his avowed mission.

But, as it turned out, Marshal Ney was not loyal to the King. He was loyal to Napoleon. After all, he was the son of a poor laborer and had risen in the ranks through many battles and many victories. It was Napoleon who had chosen a wife for him and arranged his marriage. It was Napoleon who had raised him to the rank of general and then to marshal. And Napoleon had also conferred on him the title of duke and later the title of prince. Poor boys do not often rise to become princes of an empire. Ney was grateful to his benefactor and when he marched his great body of troops out of Paris, in spite of his promise to the King, he was marching to join Napoleon.

Exactly seventeen days after Napoleon had landed on the coast of France, his troops met those of Marshal Ney. They came together in an open field. Napoleon walked forward and embraced his faithful old marshal. And the men cheered them and cried, "Long live the Emperor!"

Two days later Napoleon entered the palace at Fontainebleau. It was here that, less than a year before, he had signed his abdication. Here he had said farewell to his Old Guard on the day he left for exile. But now he was back.

* * *

The fast dispatch riders from Paris took over a week to reach Vienna.

The news of Napoleon's escape from Elba, and his landing in southern France, burst upon the Congress like a bombshell. In the confusion that followed, only three decisions were reached: Napoleon was declared an outlaw; he was to be arrested at once; his penalty was to be death before a firing squad.

It took another week for the dispatch riders to bring these orders back to Paris. By that time Napoleon had marched triumphantly through France and had reached Fontainebleau, only thirty-seven miles outside the French capital.

Napoleon stayed only one night in Fontainebleau. Early the next morning he and his army started toward Paris.

When they entered Paris, Louis XVIII had fled. He had been awakened in the dead of night and told to waste no time in leaving the Tuileries. He was frightened; for he remembered only too well what had happened to his brother, and his carriage did not stop, except to change horses, until it had crossed the border into

Holland. He sought refuge in a foreign land because he knew, now that Napoleon had returned, there was not a place in France where he would be safe.

*   *   *

Napoleon's ride from Fontainebleau to the Tuileries in Paris was a triumphant one.

Once more he rode at the head of his army surrounded by his old marshals and generals. Once more the people lined the way, welcoming him.

When he reached the palace he was hailed by huge, happy crowds that had thronged into the gardens to await his arrival. Once again he heard the people of Paris acclaim him. Again and again he heard the resounding cry of "Long live the Emperor! Long live the Emperor!"

Then, entering his old palace, he was almost crushed by joyous friends who crowded about him. Some in their enthusiasm lifted him to their shoulders and carried him up the great marble staircase to the apartments above. Others followed behind, shouting and laughing. It was a happy moment.

Here he was welcomed by many of his former ministers of state and by some of the jeweled ladies of his old court. He went from one to the other, greeting each in turn. He was truly glad to see his old friends again and be back in the familiar palace rooms.

He wandered about the apartments of his old home,

going from room to room; and in every room he entered he found the titled ladies of his court busy rearranging things. They were hurriedly removing all the Bourbon fleurs-de-lis and replacing them with Napoleon's emblem —bees. In one room he surprised a number of ladies sitting on the floor sewing cloth bees over fleurs-de-lis on a large palace carpet!

When he entered his personal rooms, he found the bed still unmade. During the last twenty-four hours, events had occurred so rapidly that no one had found time to make the bed which the frightened Louis XVIII had left so hurriedly.

It was just twenty days since Napoleon had sailed from Elba with a handful of troops. Now he was in the Tuileries, once more the Emperor of France and leader of her army. But he could not waste time celebrating and rejoicing.

He knew only too well that every ruler of Europe was pitted against him. He knew that once more he would have to face their combined armies; he would have to fight to defend his throne. He, therefore, set to work at once organizing the country for the conflict which he knew was to come.

Now began that period, crowded with events, which is known in history as The Hundred Days. During these Hundred Days, history was made and unmade. And the destiny of the world hung in the balance.

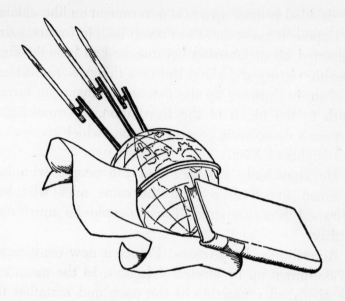

XII

THE HUNDRED DAYS

Napoleon had been in exile a little less than a year. Now
he was back in Paris and, once more, Emperor.

During his exile France had been occupied by foreign
troops and her government had been under the authority
of the conquerors. Defeat had changed the temper of the
people, and Napoleon quickly recognized this. To regain
their full support and to instill in them the spirit necessary to fight the enemies who were pitted against him,

159

he decided to draw up a new government on liberal lines.

Napoleon knew that the French had, in former years, tolerated his dictatorship because he had brought them wealth, victory and glory. But now things were different and so, in drawing up the new government, he turned back to the ideals of the Revolution. He would give France a democratic government, one which recognized the Rights of Man.

He knew only too well that the people who had stormed the Bastille were the same ones who had crowned him Emperor. These people he must now satisfy.

Accordingly, he promised France a new constitution to be drawn up by elected delegates. In the meantime he abolished censorship of the press and curtailed the powers of the police. He created a house of representatives, the members of which were to be elected by the people. The judicial department was reorganized and trial by jury was instituted for all criminal cases. And Negro slavery and slave traffic were abolished from France and all her possessions. Napoleon had the vision to take this step eighteen years before slavery was abolished in the British Dominions and forty years before it was abolished in the United States.

These changes, as well as numerous others, were immediately instituted. Napoleon felt that they complied with the spirit of the time, and that they would help the people recapture some of the zeal of the Revolution.

This was the spirit he needed for combating his enemies.

To celebrate the adoption of the new Constitution and his return to power, Napoleon planned a dazzling public ceremony. He dreamed of a pageant where he would crown his little son King of Rome and his wife, Marie Louise, Empress of France. But Marie Louise and his little boy were in Vienna and the Austrian emperor would not allow them to leave.

Napoleon tried in many ways to persuade his father-in-law to change his mind, but the Emperor was firm. However, his longing for his son was so great that he finally plotted to kidnap the child and bring him back to France. But the plot was discovered before it could be carried out.

Now he would have to celebrate alone. He, therefore, decided on a new plan. Since France was beset with enemies and since there were certain to be days of war ahead, he turned the celebration into a great military spectacle displaying the patriotism and might of France.

* * *

The defeats in Russia and Germany and the lonely days on Elba had shaken Napoleon's self-confidence. His dramatic march to Paris had somewhat restored his assurance. It had bolstered his spirit, but he had lost his old energy and daring. He had aged and he found it hard to make decisions. His face was lined and he now felt so uncertain of himself that he engaged Talma, a famous actor, to teach him how to behave in a royal manner and appear like a real Emperor.

He had lost his sense of caution, and even the Royalist plots, which were constantly being uncovered, did not seem to alarm him. It was with effort that he faced the tremendous problems before him. In former years he would have solved them easily; he would have faced them as a challenge. Now they became a duty.

However, each day he worked on plans for the defense of France. He knew that before long his enemies would be gathering their forces and marching against him.

He calculated the strength of the enemy: Austria would have an army of three hundred thousand, Russia two hundred twenty-five thousand and Prussia two hundred thirty-six thousand. To these forces would be added the armies of the German states, and of Holland and England. All in all, the nations of Europe would soon be marching a million men against him.

In order to meet such a force Napoleon had to rebuild the military might of France. He at once called into service every able-bodied man in the land. He conscripted retired veterans and raked even the smallest hamlet for fresh recruits.

He ordered all kinds of military supplies: cannons, muskets, ammunition, clothing and a hundred other things. Factories were converted overnight to the pro-

duction of war goods. Blacksmith shops were commandeered for the making of gun barrels and other necessary
iron parts. And thousands of horses were requisitioned
and brought in from the farms.

At the end of two months Napoleon had a hurriedly
equipped army of three hundred seventy-five thousand.
But this was far from the million men that his enemies
would hurl against him. Therefore, he once more sought
a weakness in his enemy which he could turn to his own
advantage.

He found that the Austrian and Russian armies were
still at the far end of Europe. If he were to conquer
the British under Wellington and the Prussians under
Blücher in Belgium without delay, he would greatly
reduce the strength of his enemy. Only by defeating his
enemies one at a time could he hope to be victorious in
the end. Besides, if Belgium were reconquered, French
morale would be greatly bolstered. Such a move would
have still one more advantage: it would free the northern
border of France and allow him to concentrate his forces
on the German border to meet the oncoming Austrians
and Russians. He, therefore, decided to strike at once.

On the eleventh of June, 1815, he left the Tuileries
and drove in his carriage toward the Belgian border to
join his army which had been sent on ahead. Here he
would measure his military genius and strength against
that of Wellington and Blücher.

❀　　❀　　❀

Napoleon's forces met those of the English and Prussians in the open country a short distance outside of the city of Brussels. They met at a place called Waterloo.

Wellington chose Waterloo as the battleground because he considered it the best position from which to defend the city of Brussels, his army headquarters. Besides, Brussels was the capital of Belgium and he did not want it to fall into French hands.

Therefore, on the fifteenth of June, hearing of the approach of the French, Wellington ordered his troops to leave the city and take up positions at Waterloo. Here they were to be joined by Prussian forces under Blücher, which were twenty miles away, and numerous English divisions which were scattered about the countryside.

The scattered English divisions managed to join Wellington's army at Waterloo, but the Prussians under Blücher were attacked by the French before they could reach the battlefield.

Napoleon had planned on using his favorite tactic against Blücher and Wellington. He would divide and conquer. Therefore, when he learned of their intention to join forces against him at Waterloo, he quickly threw a wedge in between them. He hurled his full weight against Blücher's forces. At the same time he engaged the English in a diverting action with some light divisions which he had sent ahead toward Waterloo.

This maneuver proved as successful as it had many

times in the past. By sundown the English had lost the engagement and the Prussians were forced to retreat, leaving twenty thousand dead and wounded on the field.

Napoleon now sent Marshal Grouchy in pursuit of the Prussians. He was ordered to turn their retreat into a rout, while the main force of the French would swing around and engage the English at Waterloo.

On this first day, victory was his. Napoleon sent bulletins to Paris announcing the smashing defeats the enemy had suffered.

But suddenly luck turned against Napoleon. It began to rain. All night long it rained, soaking the countryside and turning the roads to mud. In the darkness the Prussians escaped the pursuing French forces under Grouchy. They retreated in three separate sections and in three different directions. Then before dawn, safe from the French, they once more rejoined each other.

In the middle of the night Marshal Grouchy sent Napoleon a message saying that the Prussians had completely eluded him and that he despaired of locating them. But Napoleon, feeling certain that the Prussians were fleeing in terror, and eager to continue with his original plan, ordered the attack on the English to begin the following morning. And so all night the tired French forces marched through the rain and mud to Waterloo and took up their battle positions.

The next day was Sunday. The rain stopped in the morning and, as the mist lifted, Napoleon saw Wellington's forces drawn up on the opposite hill. His line was about a mile long, and only three quarters of a mile of open fields separated it from the French army. Napoleon was happy.

"At last!" he exclaimed. "At last I have the English in my grasp."

But Napoleon did not know that during the night Wellington himself had ridden out into the dark in search of Blücher. He had found him and, explaining his desperate position, had asked for immediate help. Blücher promised to send his forces back into battle immediately. He would leave only one division behind to occupy the pursuing French if they should appear. The rest of his men would march to Waterloo.

*　　*　　*

Napoleon had hoped to open fire at nine o'clock in the morning. But the ground was too wet to bring the artillery into action, and too wet for the horses of the cavalry divisions.

He was unable to begin the battle before noon. All this time the British waited patiently for his attack. After an opening salvo from his cannon, Napoleon swung his cavalry against Wellington's right wing. But the English quickly formed into squares and waited for the men and horses to come within ten yards before they opened fire. The murderous fire from hundreds of English muskets soon forced the French back; and the French cavalry retreated, leaving behind many dead and wounded.

A second attempt to break the English line was made in the very center. Here the French infantry came into action. The men fought hand to hand with swords and bayonets. The empty breaches, on both sides, were filled with fresh troops who walked over their own dead. But no ground was gained by either side, and once more the French were forced to retire.

A third attempt was again leveled at Wellington's right. This time the French cavalry charged English artillery-men, who were manning thirty large cannon, and drove them from their positions. Then they charged into the English infantry squares, but once more English muskets brought their horses to the ground. And the greater part of this courageous French force was destroyed.

In this way the battle raged all afternoon. The losses on both sides were extremely heavy. Before evening the field was covered with ten thousand English and fifteen thousand French dead. At one time in the failing light Wellington looked out from his position on a knoll and asked his aide, "What square of mine is that out there?"

"Sir, that was your square. They are no more."

The men had fallen, killed, in formation.

Napoleon, weighing his losses, knew that he must win before darkness fell or he would never win at all.

All his forces were engaged in action except his Old Guard. These hardened veterans he had reserved in case of serious trouble. He now called them forward. He had held them back for the decisive moment. Now that moment had arrived.

The Old Guard formed into two columns and awaited the signal for their assault to begin. But, before sending them out, Napoleon laid down a barrage of cannon fire all along the enemy line. When this barrage started, however, the English troops were ordered to lie flat on the ground. The cannon fire roared over them, leaving them untouched. When the Old Guard finally charged, the English rose to their feet and opened a merciless fire against them. The Old Guard fought back and the battle raged on and on.

Wellington, seeing the Old Guard come into battle, realized that Napoleon had now used up all his troops. This was good news. But would the English be able to hold out much longer? Their reserves were also used up. For hours Wellington's men had been holding on by sheer desperation, waiting for the relief Blücher had promised. Where were the Prussians? Why were they so long in coming? Would they never arrive? If they did not come soon, the English would be forced to surrender. They could not hold out much longer.

Then in the twilight, while the Old Guard was making a last attempt to smash the English line, the Prussians arrived at Waterloo. Napoleon discovered Blücher's columns emerging from the woods on his right. He had counted on these woods for protection. He had believed that Blücher's troops were in wild retreat; and now here they were, attacking his right wing in a force strong enough to turn the tide of battle.

All afternoon the English, awaiting Blücher's arrival, had been content to hold their ground. They had fought a defensive action while the French had attacked. But now, with the arrival of the Prussian forces, they charged forward.

"All is lost!" cried Napoleon when he saw the English advancing. Spurring his horse, he dashed off the field.

His soldiers, realizing their hopeless position, threw down their guns and with cries of "Save yourselves!" broke ranks and ran. The English and Prussians charged into the panic-stricken French troops. The confusion and slaughter continued until darkness fell.

Thus ended the bloody battle of Waterloo.

The English lost fifteen thousand dead and wounded of their original seventy thousand men. Of Napoleon's force of seventy-four thousand, over forty thousand were lost. And Blücher lost seven thousand of his ninety thousand. All in all, sixty-two thousand men fell at Waterloo. And, in an area which covered only three square miles of the battleground, there were piled more than forty-five thousand dead, thousands of dead horses, three thousand shattered French cannons and uncounted wrecked wagons. Death and ruin were everywhere.

This was Waterloo. Here on a Sunday afternoon Napoleon fought his last battle. The French army was crushed. And, from this day on, the word Waterloo became a synonym for defeat.

Napoleon, shaken and filled with fear, had left the battlefield. He did not check his racing horse until he was several miles away. Here, alone in the dark, with the sounds of battle behind him in the distance, he tried to collect his thoughts. He tried to clear the scene of Waterloo from his mind. He tried to think of what he should do. To return to his troops on the battlefield was impossible. He could have overlooked the agony of blood and death of even a million of his men if their sacrifice had brought him victory. But defeat . . .

He rode on through the night, alone. What should he now do? Then suddenly he decided to do as he had done four times before. He would rush back alone to Paris before the news of his crushing defeat reached the city. He urged his horse on, and all night long he rode southward.

Just before dawn, as he neared the town of Philippeville, he was overtaken by a group of his officers. They, too, had left the men on the field of battle.

At Philippeville, Napoleon commandeered three carriages to take him and his aides to Paris. He rode alone in the first. His officers followed behind in the other two.

This was the fourth time that Napoleon had deserted his army. Each time he had done so when faced with defeat. In the early days he had left his troops stranded in Egypt and secretly returned to Paris. Later, during the retreat from Moscow he had also abandoned them. At Leipzig he had run from the field of battle, and now he was fleeing from Waterloo. Each time he had rushed back to Paris.

As Napoleon's carriage rolled on, the people of Paris were celebrating the victories he had announced after the first day of battle. The dispatches he had sent in the night had reached Paris and the city was jubilant. They thought that the glory of France was secure. Once more Napoleon was their savior, their idol. A hundred cannon roared a salute in his honor. And thousands of voices cried, "Long live the Emperor!"

*　　*　　*

Alone that night, after the city was asleep, Napoleon's carriage arrived at the Tuileries. No welcoming crowd greeted him. His return was unexpected.

He walked wearily up the marble staircase to his private apartment. He knew that at this very moment Wellington and Blücher were certain to be marching their troops toward Paris. With the French army shattered, he could offer no resistance. By morning the full news of Waterloo would reach Paris. Faced with these inescapable facts, Napoleon knew that there was only one thing for him to do—abdicate.

He went to his desk and picked up his pen. He wrote the bitter words.

*　　*　　*

Napoleon's abdication was accepted by a delegation from the Senate. With this abdication the famous Hundred Days came to an end.

As a private citizen, Napoleon left the Tuileries for the last time and moved to his old home on the *Rue de la Victoire*. It was here that he and Josephine had lived before moving to the Tuileries. Now Josephine was dead, and Marie Louise and his son were in Vienna. He was alone and defeated.

The members of his family advised him to leave France without delay. English and Prussian forces were already on French soil. Soon the armies of the Czar and the Austrians would join them. If he did not leave at once, he would surely be taken prisoner.

Napoleon found it hard to leave the land and people that he loved. For several days he postponed making a decision. He kept hoping for a miracle. But at length he was persuaded by his friends that he must make his escape. It was decided that he should hurry to the coast of France and take a ship to America. Many friends, professing their loyalty, offered to accompany him.

And so it was that, several days later, a long line of carriages left Paris for the Atlantic port of Rochefort. They carried Napoleon, his close companions, their wives, children, servants and baggage. At Rochefort the party was to board two French frigates and sail for America.

Napoleon left Paris on a Saturday night. Exactly two weeks before, on another Saturday night, he had led his men through the rain, mud and darkness to the field of Waterloo. The following morning, when the mist lifted, he had seen the English line on the opposite hill and exclaimed, "At last! At last I have the English in my grasp." This was the morning of the battle of Waterloo.

And now barely a fortnight later he was fleeing from France. He was fleeing to save his life.

❋   ❋   ❋

Had Napoleon arrived at the port of Rochefort alone, or with only one or two companions, he would surely have escaped to America. His arrival would have passed unnoticed. But with a retinue of one hundred people it was not possible. The British had been informed of his plans, and the port officials told Napoleon that three British ships under the command of the man-of-war *Bellerophone* were guarding the harbor and ready to search all departing vessels. It would be impossible for the two French frigates to slip through this blockade.

In the meantime, reports came to Napoleon that Paris was occupied by the enemies and that the Bourbon King, Louis XVIII, was again being brought back to the throne. In many parts of France the Royalists were assuming power and the Bourbon flag was again flying. Escape by crossing the interior of France to the Mediterranean coast was now also impossible. Napoleon felt that the wisest thing for him to do was to surrender to Captain Maitland of the British man-of-war. He, therefore, notified the captain of his intention. A barge from the *Bellerophone* was sent to bring him to the man-of-war.

Dressed in his uniform, which he had not worn since he left the Tuileries, Napoleon with a few companions stepped aboard the barge, and the British sailors began to row him out into the harbor. His friends, with tears in their eyes, watched him leave. They tried to encourage him by cheering. They cheered as long as he was still in sight.

As Napoleon mounted the quarter-deck of the *Bellerophone*, he addressed Captain Maitland. "I come to place myself under the protection of your prince and laws."

The anchor was weighed; the sails were unfurled and the British man-of-war sailed out of the harbor. Napoleon stood at the rail and watched the coastline as it receded into the distance. He watched it sadly and as long as it remained in sight. In his heart he knew that this was the last time he would ever see France.

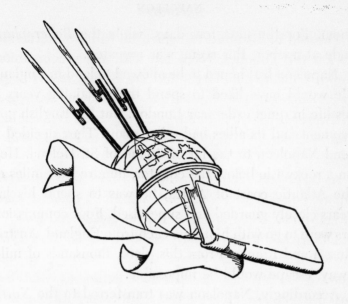

XIII

ST. HELENA

When the *Bellerophone* anchored off the coast of southern England, the news that Napoleon was a captive on board was already known. Hundreds of little boats—rowboats, fishing yawls, sailboats—swarmed about the man-of-war. They carried crowds of people curious to see Napoleon. He was obliging and several times appeared on deck. He was greeted by the cheers of the people. He acknowledged their cheers by waving to them. For the next few days, while the *Bellerophone* rode at anchor, this scene was repeated.

Napoleon had hoped to be allowed to land in England. He would have liked to spend the remaining years of his life in quiet exile near London. But the English government and its allies had other plans. They decided to send Napoleon to the far-off island of St. Helena. Here on a rocky isle below the equator, hundreds of miles off the Atlantic coast of Africa, he was to spend his last years closely guarded and supervised. Four commissioners were to go with him: one each from England, Austria, Russia and France. From this place, thousands of miles away, escape would be impossible.

Accordingly, Napoleon was transferred to the *Northumberland*, a British man-of-war. He was allowed to take with him into exile four companions, a doctor and twelve servants. The *Northumberland* set sail accompanied by two frigates and seven brigs, and after a journey of over a month it anchored in the small harbor of Jamestown, St. Helena, on October 15, 1815.

Napoleon and his party came ashore and were taken into the country to a simple one-story house called Longwood.

* * *

Napoleon tried hard to accommodate himself to his exile.

He attempted to follow his old routine. He rose early each day, took a short walk and then came back to Longwood to work. He dictated many letters and each day he worked on his memoirs. He was eager to leave the world a full account of his personal life, his campaigns and his political accomplishments. He plunged into this work with great earnestness, but he had few papers and reference works to remind him of the accurate details. He remembered mainly the moments of his glory and he brushed aside most of his failures. He tried to avoid the disagreeable and he often cast blame on others.

On reflection he felt that it was "the ulcer of Spain and the Austrian princess" that caused his downfall. These, he recorded, were the two great mistakes of his life. He should have conquered Spain before launching upon the Russian campaign. As for his wife, Marie Louise, he wrote, "There I stepped into an abyss covered with flowers."

* * *

Napoleon accepted the first two years of his exile with fortitude. In time, however, the daily irritations of life on St. Helena began to undermine his health.

He who had once ruled an Empire was now confined to a narrow existence. His daily companions were the four friends who had come into exile with him. They began to tire of one another. The English commissioner was unnecessarily harsh and petty toward him. Among the many regulations he imposed was one which humiliated Napoleon. He was to be addressed as "General Bonaparte," not as "Emperor." The many letters he wrote to his beloved little son in Austria remained unanswered.

Napoleon began to complain of ill health. He suffered from indigestion and swollen legs. The medicines the doctor gave him did little good, but he still found energy to work on his memoirs.

A year later he abandoned this work. A marked decline set in and he found no pleasure in recalling the past. Several of his companions left him to return to Europe. All in all, life on the rocky island was becoming more and more desolate. He was lonely and sad.

He began to think of death and he dictated his will. This is a long and curious document. In it he remembered all who had been faithful to him. He bequeathed to them generously, even estates, money and holdings which he knew had long ago been confiscated by the Bourbons.

This will also contains one last request. "I wish that my ashes may rest on the banks of the Seine, in the midst of the people I so greatly loved."

* * *

Toward the end of 1820, just five years after Waterloo, Napoleon became seriously ill. He took to his bed. It was now evident that he was suffering from cancer of the stomach, but the disease had progressed so far that an operation was impossible.

In the spring of the following year, on May 5, 1821, Napoleon died. He was fifty-one years old. His request that he be buried in France was not granted by the English governor. He was buried in a simple grave on the island of his exile, St. Helena.

*　　*　　*

During the years that followed, time cooled the resentment and hatred that Europe felt for Napoleon. And the people of France turned affectionately to his memory.

Twenty years after his death the French government, under the pressure of public desire, asked England and her allies if his body might be brought to France. When consent was granted, the French sent a battleship to St. Helena to bring home the remains of the man who had once been their Emperor.

They were bringing home the Corsican who as a child had come to France, the Little Corporal who had risen in the ranks. They were bringing home the general who had dragged his cannon through the tropical sands of Egypt and over the icy peaks of the Alps, the man who had conquered most of Europe and humbled princes and kings. They were bringing home the man who had led France to overwhelming victories and shattering defeats, who had lost a whole army in the snows of Russia. Now, at last, the Emperor—he who had escaped from Elba and marched to Paris to snatch back the throne from the Bourbons and fight the enemy at Waterloo—was coming home. They would place his remains, as he had wished, "on the banks of the Seine."

Napoleon's coffin was carried in a solemn procession through Paris to the *Invalides,* a building "on the banks of the Seine," where it rests today "in the midst of the people I so greatly loved." The city had never before been moved so deeply.

He who had been banished and died in exile had now returned. He who had lived by the motto "I command or else I am silent" was now at peace.

His name, Napoleon, is burned like a brand into the pages of history.

BIBLIOGRAPHY

De Chair, Somerset (Editor)
Napoleon's Memoirs
Harper & Bros., New York, 1949.

Richardson, H. N. B.
A Dictionary of Napoleon and His Times
Funk and Wagnalls, New York.

Guérard, Albert Leon
Reflections on the Napoleonic Legend
Charles Scribner's Sons, New York, 1924.

Thompson, J. M. (Translator and Editor)
Napoleon Self-Revealed in 300 Selected Letters
Houghton Mifflin Co., Boston, 1934.

De Bourrienne, Louis A. F.
Memoirs of Napoleon Bonaparte by His Private Secretary (4 vols.)
Charles Scribner's Sons, New York, 1890.

The Cambridge Modern History
Napoleon Vol. IX
(Contains a fine bibliography of 120 pp.)
The Macmillan Co., New York, 1907.

Pratt, Fletcher
The Empire and the Glory, Napoleon Bonaparte: 1800-1806
William Sloane Associates, Inc., New York, 1949.

Ludwig, Emil
Napoleon
Boni & Liveright, New York, 1926.

Sloane, William Milligan
The Life of Napoleon Bonaparte (4 vols.)
New York, 1939.

Lockhart, John Gibson
The History of Napoleon Buonaparte
E. P. Dutton & Co., New York, 1829.

Kircheisen, F. M.
Napoleon
Harcourt, Brace & Co., New York, 1932.

INDEX

183

About the Author

MANUEL KOMROFF was born in New York City, and educated in schools there and at Yale. He worked as a newspaper man and during World War I as a war correspondent. His first short stories appeared in 1918, and since then one hundred and thirty of them have been published. He is also the author of many adult novels and biographies of famous historical personages for young people. For a number of years he lectured at Columbia University where he conducted a Novel Writing Workshop. He is a member of the Author's Guild, P.E.N., the Overseas Press Club.